Ordnance Survey

Mid Wales and the Marches Walks

Pathfinder Guide

Compiled by Laurence Main
Series editor: Brian Conduit

Key to colour coding

The walks are divided into three broad categories, indicated by the following colours:

Short, easy walks

Walks of moderate length, likely to involve some uphill walking

More challenging walks, which may be longer and/or over more rugged terrain, often with some stiff climbs

Acknowledgements

I should like to thank Letty Rowan, George Wemyss, Janet Davies, Richard Edwards and the Reverend Jim McKnight, who were kind enough to drive me to some of the walks, and Jeremy Moore for taking most of the photographs. I also wish to thank J.D. Lewis & Son Limited, Gomer Press, Llandysul, for permission to quote the English translation of St David's last words from *Candle in the Darkness*; to thank Kent State University Press, Ohio, USA, for permission to quote part of the English translation by Rolfe Humphries of the poem 'Merched Llanbadarn' (The Girls of Llanbadarn) by Dafydd ap Gwilym from *Nine Thorny Thickets* (1969); and to acknowledge Joseph P. Clancy's English translation of the poem 'Elegy for Llywelyn ap Gruffudd' by Gruffudd ap yr Ynad Coch from *The Earliest Welsh Poetry, Medieval Welsh Lyrics* (Macmillan).

While every care has been taken to ensure the accuracy of the route directions, the publishers cannot accept responsibility for errors or omissions, or for changes in details given. It has to be emphasised that the countryside is not static: hedges and fences can be removed, field boundaries can alter, footpaths can be rerouted and changes of ownership can result in the closure or diversion of some concessionary paths. Also paths that are easy and pleasant for walking in fine conditions may become slippery, muddy and difficult in wet weather and stepping stones over rivers and streams may become impassable. If readers know of any changes which have taken place, or have noticed any inaccuracies, Jarrold Publishing would be grateful to hear from them.

Ordnance Survey   ISBN 0-319-00486-4
Jarrold Publishing   ISBN 0-7117-0818-5

First published 1995 by Ordnance Survey and Jarrold Publishing

Ordnance Survey   Jarrold Publishing
Romsey Road   Whitefriars
Southampton SO16 4GU   Norwich NR3 1TR

© Crown copyright 1995

Printed in Great Britain by Jarrold Printing, Norwich. 1/95

Previous page: *Cottages at Clun*

Contents

Introduction to mid Wales and the Marches

These are the forgotten lands, at the back of beyond. Rural, unspoilt, sparsely populated and eternally peaceful, they await discovery by the discerning, thoughtful, pedestrian tourist. Forgotten by the planners when the national parks were created, the consequent lack of attention has added to the appeal of these areas. Overshadowed by Snowdonia to the north and the Brecon Beacons to the south, mid Wales is a 'green desert', which has acted as a formidable barrier between North and South Wales. Shrouded by Celtic mists, it baffled the advance of the English invaders, thus preserving the Welsh language in the west of Wales.

Not all of mid Wales escaped anglicisation. The border between Celt and Saxon was the River Severn in AD 603, when the British bishops met St Augustine. The old Kingdom of Powys (the name derives from *pagenses*, the Latin for 'country-dwellers') had its capital at Pengwern, near Shrewsbury. By the end of the eighth century the Welsh were kept to the west of Offa's Dyke. The Marches represent further inroads into Wales made by the Normans. The 'lost territory' on the eastern side of the modern frontier still has an air of Welshness.

Mid Wales

Every country must have its holy mountain, and Plynlimon serves that purpose at the heart of Wales. Its lonely summit is surrounded by a sea of moorland that seems to isolate it from the sophisticated world. It is still necessary to drive around this upland rather than go through it. The people who live around Plynlimon may be the direct descendants of those who retreated here in the Old Stone Age. They are dark, long-headed with broad cheekbones and have a high proportion of the pre-B blood group.

At first sight these uplands seem unable to sustain much life, whether of the human or wild variety. Investigation suggests that it has provided sanctuary for the rare types. Perhaps their standard-bearer is the red kite. This bird of prey used to clean up London when drains and sewers were left open. Savage persecution meant that only three pairs were left in the whole of Great Britain by 1900. They clung to existence in mid Wales. Now encouraged by conservationists, they are growing in numbers, and it would be remarkable if you did not spot at least one in the course of walking the routes in this book.

Buzzards are plentiful, yet remain a majestic sight. Go for a walk on a fine day and you will probably see several, especially over woodland. Go to the lakes and bogs, such as the Teifi Pools (Walk 27) to spot dunlin and golden plover.

The natural lakes have been supplemented by artificial reservoirs, as in the Elan valley. Mid Wales is rich in water, and great rivers flow from here. The Severn makes its regal way to and through England. The source of the Wye is also on Plynlimon, and this delightful river strays into the Marches territory that is now in England, before completing its journey along the modern border and feeding into the Severn estuary.

The 'green desert' has been planted with conifer trees in places, but if nature had its way this would be mainly oak woodland. Centuries of clearing the natural vegetation was accelerated by the introduction of sheep-farming by the Cistercians and the strategic removal of potential cover for hostile Welsh by the invading Normans and English in the Middle Ages. Some oak trees have survived on hillsides too steep for the plough. Birch and rowan accompany them on the acidic, boggy, upland soils. Ash, wych-elm, hazel, holly, hawthorn, sycamore and alder join the oak on lime-rich soils, as found south-east of Builth.

Early man must have used the uplands more than the wooded valleys. The Kerry Ridgeway (Walk 25) was an important route from the earliest days. Physical evidence of prehistoric peoples in the form of standing stones, burial chambers and stone circles can be found, but the really intriguing relics are the legends. When, for instance, was the drowning of Cantre'r Gwaelod and what is Sarn Gynfelyn? Folk memory could extend to 3500 BC around Borth (Walk 9). The two long-horned oxen of Llanddewi-Brefi (Walk 2) may date from the Age of Taurus (approximately 4000–2000 BC), since the Hu Gadarn of the legend is also John Bull. Professor Alexander Thom, author of *Megalithic Sites in Britain* (Oxford, 1967), regarded a stone circle near Kerry as one of the three most important such sites in Britain. Its compound ring design would seem to have inspired the construction of Avebury.

The early sites may have been sacred in nature, but by the Iron Age (from around 600 BC) hilltop communities, as on Pen Dinas above Aberystwyth (Walk 9), needed defensive fortifications. They did not help much against the might of the Roman legions. Caradoc (or Cara[c]tacus,

The Ithon valley and Cambrian Mountains from the high ground above Llandrindod

died *c.* 54) made his last stand somewhere near Knighton. However, Rome was never fully in control of this part of the world, despite erecting camps at strategic points, such as Caersws, and building roads or improving existing British routes. Pumsaint's Dolaucothi mines, not far from the location of Walk 1 (Twm Siôn Catti's Cave), were exploited by the Romans for gold. Similarly, a small Roman fort on Penycrocbren guarded the lead mines of Dylife, not far from Wynford Vaughan Thomas' Viewpoint (Walk 18).

When the legions departed, Wales enjoyed the golden age of the Celtic saints. One of these was female, St Erfyl. Her tombstone is housed in the church at the end of Walk 12 (Llanerfyl). The most famous of these saints is David or Dewi, the patron saint of Wales, who settled arguments at Llanddewi-Brefi (Walk 2). Traditionally, the synod here in 519 was called to deal with the Pelagian heresy, which taught that men had no need of God's grace. Pelagius may have preached his first heretical sermon at Castle Caereinion (Walk 5), which was visited by the French bishop Germanus in 429. Imagine the long arm of the Vatican some 1500 years before the Welshpool & Llanfair Light Railway served this remote village!

Rome lost its grip on the Celtic Church and when St Augustine came to preach to the English in 597, the Welsh did not support his mission. This was because the arrogant Augustine remained seated when the Celtic Church delegates came into his presence. If he had stood up to greet them, the course of history may have been different.

When the Welsh were finally losing their married clergy in the Middle Ages, the Cistercians were arriving to change the landscape as well as erect beautiful buildings at Abbeycwmhir and Strata Florida. The headless body of the last true native Prince of Wales was buried at Abbeycwmhir in 1282. Llywelyn the Last came from the mountain stronghold of Gwynedd to assert Welsh independence in Powys. Being closer to England, Powys had learnt to cushion and absorb the demands of the English rather than attempt to repel them, so it sided with the English against Gwynedd. Indeed, Llywelyn the Last was also the First because national unity was not a Welsh concept.

With the exception of Owain Glyndŵr's bold drive for an independent Wales in the early fifteenth century, Welsh history now merged with that of England. The two nations were united under the Tudors by the Acts of Union in 1535 and 1536, with English becoming the sole official language. The Welsh-speakers found employment in the metal mines, especially to the south-east of Aberystwyth.

A lasting legacy of the mines has been the Vale of Rheidol Railway. The Heart of Wales line brought Victorian visitors to the area, rather than minerals out. Actually, they came for the minerals – the mineral water. The heyday of the largest of the spas, at Llandrindod Wells (Walk 16), is re-created at the end of every August, when the town dresses up in Victorian costumes.

Sheep pasture dominates the landscape but more and more land is being planted with conifer forests, while windmills are being erected to form energy farms. All these aspects of modern mid Wales can be seen along the walks in this book.

The Marches

This tranquil borderland was fought over for centuries. If Glyndŵr's tripartite alliance had succeeded, the Welsh border would have returned to the River Severn as far east as Worcester. Most of the old Marcher lordships were contained within Wales after the Acts of Union, but parts of

5

Marcher territory were added to the English counties of Shropshire, Herefordshire and Gloucestershire.

Mention Herefordshire and Alfred Watkins comes to mind. His book *The Old Straight Track* (1925) reflects his intimate knowledge of this area. It also introduced the concept of leys to modern Britain. One ley in his book clips the corner of Sutton Walls (Walk 17). The word 'march' is possibly derived from the Old English *mearc*, which is linked with leys as well as with boundaries.

With its varied landscape truncated by rivers meandering to lowland plains, this area where Wales merges with England has great appeal to the rambler. Limestone to the west and north of the old red sandstone of the Hereford Plain has given rise to exceptionally attractive hilly country with delightfully narrow valleys.

Walking in the area

Walking in mid Wales and the Marches is a rewarding experience, enhanced by the sense of isolation and the awareness of a rich history. Thinly populated open moorland attracts the wanderer, and within the gathering grounds of the Elan valley reservoirs the walker is invited to ramble freely – indeed this right was secured by Act of Parliament. Sheep pasture demands fences, and gates or stiles are not always in place, while dogs are never welcome. Canine companions are more suited to the forest track, well away from sheep.

More and more paths are being waymarked and provided with what is termed

Borth and the Dyfi valley

'footpath furniture' – stiles and gates. No doubt access would be easier if the area was not so big and the population density so low. More people live in Oxford than in the whole of Powys! But the charm of mid Wales is its 'green desert' nature. In future the area may come to value its rights of way more, if only as sources of income from tourists. If you follow a waymarked national trail like the Offa's Dyke Path, the potential in pedestrian tourism should become obvious, especially on a sunny summer day, when everybody seems to be out discovering the joys of walking. The Wye Valley Walk and Glyndŵr's Way generate similar trade. Other recognised long-distance routes through the area include the Marches Way, linking Chester with Cardiff, the Shropshire Way, which is followed for a while on Walk 26 (Clun), the Cambrian Way, running between Cardiff and Conwy, and the Dyfi Valley Way, which ends at Borth (Walk 19).

Glossary of Welsh words

aber	estuary, confluence
afon	river
bach, fach	small
bont, pont	bridge
bryn	mound, hill
bwlch	pass
caer	fort
capel	chapel
carn, carnedd	cairn
castell	castle
ceunant	gorge, ravine
coed	wood
craig	crag
crib	narrow ridge
cwm	cirque, valley
drws	door, gap (pass)
dyffryn	valley
eglwys, llan	church
fach, bach	small
fawr, mawr	big, large
ffordd	road
foel, moel	rounded hill
fynydd, mynydd	mountain
glyn	glen
hen	old
llan, eglwys	church
llwybr	path
llyn	lake
maen	stone
maes	field
mawr, fawr	big, large
moel, foel	rounded hill

The memorial stone to Llywelyn the Last, Cilmeri

morfa	sea marsh
mynydd, fynydd	mountain
nant	brook, stream
newydd	new
pair	cauldron
pen	head, top
pentre(f)	village
pont, bont	bridge
pwll	pool
rhaedr	waterfall
sarn	causeway
traeth	beach, shore
tre(f), dre(f)	town
tŷ	house
twll	hole
ynys	island

The Ramblers' Association

No organisation works more actively to protect and extend the rights and interests of walkers in the countryside than the Ramblers' Association. Its aims (summarised here) are clear: to foster a greater knowledge, love and care of the countryside; to assist in the protection and enhancement of public rights of way and areas of natural beauty; to work for greater public access to the countryside; and to encourage more people to take up rambling as a healthy, recreational activity.

It was founded in 1935 when, following the setting up of a National Council of Ramblers' Federation in 1931, a number of federations earlier formed in London, Manchester, the Midlands and else-where came together to create a more effective pressure group, to deal with such contemporary problems as the disappearance and obstruction of foot-paths, the prevention of access to open mountain and moorland and increasing hostility from landowners. This was the era of the mass trespasses, when there were sometimes violent confrontations between ramblers and gamekeepers, especially on the moorlands of the Peak District.

Since then the Ramblers' Association has played an influential role in pre-serving and developing the national foot-path network, supporting the creation of national parks and encouraging the designation and waymarking of long-distance footpaths.

Our freedom to walk in the countryside is precarious, and requires constant vigilance. As well as the perennial problems of footpaths being illegally obstructed, disappearing through lack of use or extinguished by housing or road construction, new dangers can spring up at any time.

It is to meet such problems and dangers that the Ramblers' Association exists and represents the interests of all walkers. The address to write to for information on the Ramblers' Association and how to become a member is given on page 78.

Walkers and the law

Woodland walk around Dinas Nature Reserve

The average walker in a national park or other popular walking area, armed with the appropriate Ordnance Survey map, reinforced perhaps by a guidebook giving detailed walking instructions, is unlikely to run into legal difficulties, but it is useful to know something about the law relating to public rights of way. The right to walk over certain parts of the countryside has developed over a long period of time, and how such rights came into being and how far they are protected by the law is a complex subject, fascinating in its own right, but too lengthy to be discussed here. The following comments are intended simply to be a helpful guide, backed up by the Countryside Access Charter, a concise summary of walkers' rights and obligations drawn up by the Countryside Commission.

Basically there are two main kinds of public rights of way: footpaths (for walkers only) and bridleways (for walkers, riders on horseback and pedal cyclists). Footpaths and bridleways are shown by broken green lines on Ordnance Survey Pathfinder and Outdoor Leisure maps and broken red lines on Landranger maps. There is also a third category, called byways or 'roads used as a public path': chiefly broad, walled tracks (green lanes) or farm roads, which walkers, riders and cyclists have to share, usually only occasionally, with motor vehicles. Many of these public paths have been in existence for hundreds of years and some even originated as prehistoric trackways and have been in constant use for well over 2,000 years.

The term 'right of way' means exactly what it says. It gives right of passage over what, in the vast majority of cases, is private land, and you are required to keep to the line of the path and not stray onto the land either side. If you inadvertently wander off the right of way – either because of faulty map-reading or because the route is not clearly indicated on the ground – you are technically trespassing and the wisest course is to ask the nearest available person (farmer or fellow walker) to direct you back to the correct route. There are stories of unpleasant confrontations between walkers and farmers at times, but in general most farmers are helpful and co-operative when responding to a genuine and polite request for assistance in route-finding.

Obstructions can sometimes be a problem and probably the most common of these is where a path across a field has been ploughed up. It is legal for a farmer to plough up a path provided that he restores it within two weeks, barring exceptionally bad weather. This does not always happen and here the walker is presented with a dilemma: to follow the line of the path, even if this inevitably means treading on crops, or to use common sense and walk around the edge of the field. The latter course of action often seems the best but, as this means that you would be trespassing, you are, in law, supposed to keep to the exact line of the path, avoiding unnecessary damage to crops. In the case of other obstructions which may block a path (illegal fences and locked gates etc.), common sense again has to be used in order to negotiate them by the easiest method (detour or removal). If you have any problems negotiating rights of way, you should report the matter to the rights of way department of the relevant county, borough or metropolitan district council. They will then take action with the landowner concerned.

Apart from rights of way enshrined by law, there are a number of other paths available to walkers. Permissive or concessionary paths have been created where a landowner has given permission for the public to use a particular route across his land. The main problem with these is that, as they have been granted as a concession, there is no legal right to use them and therefore they can be extinguished at any time. In practice, many of these concessionary routes have been established on land owned either by large public bodies such as the Forestry Com-

- byways (usually old roads), most 'roads used as public paths' and, of course, public roads – all traffic has the right of way

Use maps, signs and waymarks to check rights of way. Ordnance Survey Pathfinder and Landranger maps show most public rights of way

On rights of way you can:
- take a pram, pushchair or wheelchair if practicable
- take a dog (on a lead or under close control)
- take a short route round an illegal obstruction or remove it sufficiently to get past

You have a right to go for recreation to:
- public parks and open spaces – on foot
- most commons near older towns and cities – on foot and sometimes on horseback
- private land where the owner has a formal agreement with the local authority

In addition you can use the following by local or established custom or consent, but ask for advice if you are unsure:
- many areas of open country, such as moorland, fell and coastal areas, especially those in the care of the National Trust, and some commons
- some woods and forests, especially those owned by the Forestry Commission
- country parks and picnic sites
- most beaches
- canal towpaths
- some private paths and tracks

Consent sometimes extends to horse-riding and cycling

For your information:
- county councils and London boroughs maintain and record rights of way, and register commons
- obstructions, dangerous animals, harassment and misleading signs on rights of way are illegal and you should report them to the county council
- paths across fields can be ploughed, but must normally be reinstated within two weeks
- landowners can require you to leave land to which you have no right of access
- motor vehicles are normally permitted only on roads, byways and some 'roads used as public paths'

mission, or by a private one, such as the National Trust, and as these mainly encourage walkers to use their paths, they are unlikely to be closed unless a change of ownership occurs.

Walkers also have free access to country parks (except where requested to keep away from certain areas for ecological reasons, e.g. wildlife protection, woodland regeneration, safe-guarding of rare plants etc.), canal towpaths and most beaches. By custom, though not by right, you are generally free to walk across the open and uncultivated higher land of mountain, moorland and fell, but this varies from area to area and from one season to another – grouse moors, for example, will be out of bounds during the breeding and shooting seasons and some open areas are used as Ministry of Defence firing ranges, for which reason access will be restricted. In some areas the situation has been clarified as a result of 'access agreements' between the landowners and either the county council or the national park authority, which clearly define when and where you can walk over such open country.

Countryside Access Charter

Your rights of way are:
- public footpaths – on foot only. Sometimes waymarked in yellow
- bridleways – on foot, horseback and pedal cycle. Sometimes waymarked in blue

Key Map 1

Key Map 2

CONVENTIONAL SIGNS   1 : 25 000 or 2½ INCHES to 1 MILE

ROADS AND PATHS
Not necessarily rights of way

M1 or A6(M)	M1 or A6(M)	Motorway
A 31(T)	A 31(T)	Trunk or Main road
B 3074	B 3074	Secondary road
A 35	A 35	Dual carriageway
		Road generally more than 4m wide
		Road generally less than 4m wide
		Other road, drive or track

Unfenced roads and tracks are shown by pecked lines
.... Path

RAILWAYS

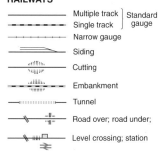

Multiple track	Standard gauge
Single track	
Narrow gauge	
Siding	
Cutting	
Embankment	
Tunnel	
Road over; road under;	
Level crossing; station	

PUBLIC RIGHTS OF WAY   Public rights of way may not be evident on the ground

} Public paths { Footpath / Bridleway

+ + + + + Byway open to all traffic
▲ ▼ ▲ ▼ ▲ Road used as a public path

DANGER AREA
Firing and test ranges in the area
Danger!
Observe warning notices

The indication of a towpath in this book does not necessarily imply a public right of way
The representation of any other road, track or path is no evidence of the existence of a right of way

BOUNDARIES

— · — · — · —	County (England and Wales)
— — — — —	District
–○– –○– –○–	London Borough
· · · · · · · · · · · · ·	Civil Parish (England)* Community (Wales)
— — — — — —	Constituency (County, Borough, Burgh or European Assembly)

Coincident boundaries are shown by the first appropriate symbol

*For Ordnance Survey purposes CountyBoundary is deemed to be the limit of the parish structure whether or not a parish area adjoins

SYMBOLS

▮ } Place	with tower	
● } of worship	with spire, minaret or dome	
+ } worship	without such additions	
▢ ▢	Building; important building	
▨ △	Glasshouse; youth hostel	
⬭	Bus or coach station	
� ⅄	Lighthouse; beacon	
△ ▲	Triangulation pillar	
. T; A; R	Telephone: public; AA; RAC	
𐙞𐙞𐙞𐙞𐙞	Sloping masonry	
---□--- pylon pole	Electricity transmission line	
○ W, Spr	Well, Spring	
⌖	Site of antiquity	
⚔ 1066	Site of battle (with date)	

Gravel pit	
Other pit or quarry	
Sand pit	
Refuse or slag heap	
Loose rock	
Outcrop	
Cliff	
Boulders	
Scree	

Water		Mud	
Sand; sand & shingle			
National Park or Forest Park Boundary			
NT	National Trust always open		
NT	National Trust limited access, observe local signs		
FC	Forestry Commission		

VEGETATION   Limits of vegetation are defined by positioning of the symbols but may be delineated also by pecks or dots

Coniferous trees	
Non-coniferous trees	
Coppice	

Orchard	
Scrub	
Marsh, reeds, saltings.	

Bracken, rough grassland }
In some areas bracken ( ) and rough grassland ( ) are shown separately

Heath

Shown collectively as rough grassland on some sheets

In some areas reeds ( ) and saltings ( ) are shown separately

HEIGHTS AND ROCK FEATURES

50 · ┐
285 · ┘ Determined by | ground survey / air survey

Surface heights are to the nearest metre above mean sea level. Heights shown close to a triangulation pillar refer to the ground level height at the pillar and not necessarily at the summit

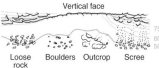

Vertical face

Loose rock　Boulders　Outcrop　Scree

75
60
50

Contours may be shown at either 5 metres or 10 metres vertical interval

TOURIST INFORMATION

✝ Abbey, Cathedral, Priory

🐟 Aquarium

⛺ Camp site

🚐 Caravan site

🏰 Castle

Cave

Country park

Craft centre

P Parking

PC Public Convenience (in rural areas)

𝔐 Ancient Monuments and Historic Buildings in the care of the Secretary of State for the Environment which are open to the public

◆────◆ National trail or Recreational Path Long Distance Route (Scotland only)

Pennine Way Named path

Garden

▶ Golf course or links

🏛 Historic house

ℹ Information centre

Motor racing

🖼 Museum

❗ Nature or forest trail

Nature reserve

✠ross
SAILING Selected places of interest

☏ T Public Telephone

⊕ Mountain rescue post

NATIONAL PARK ACCESS LAND Boundary of National Park access land Private land for which the National Park Planning Board have negotiated public access

◄ Access Point

☆ Other tourist feature

✕ Picnic site

🚂 Preserved railway

🏇 Racecourse

⛷ Skiing

Viewpoint

Wildlife park

Zoo

WALKS

 Start point of walk

Featured walk

➜ Route of walk

▪▪▶ Alternative route

ABBREVIATIONS   1 : 25 000 or 2½ INCHES to 1 MILE also 1 : 10 000/1 : 10 560 or 6 INCHES to 1 MILE

BP,BS	Boundary Post or Stone	Mon	Monument	Spr	Spring
CH	Club House	P	Post Office	T	Telephone, public
FV	Ferry Foot or Vehicle	Pol Sta	Police station	A,R	Telephone, AA or RAC
FB	Foot Bridge	PC	Public Convenience	TH	Town Hall
HO	House	PH	Public House	Twr	Tower
MP,MS	Mile Post or stone	Sch	School	W	Well
				Wd Pp	Wind Pump

Abbreviations applicable only to 1 : 10 000/1 : 10 560 or 6 INCHES to 1 MILE

Ch	Church	P	Pole or Post	TCB	Telephone Call Box
F Sta	Fire Station	PW	Place of Worship	TCP	Telephone Call Post
Fn	Fountain	S	Stone	Y	Youth Hostel
GP	Guide Post				

FOLLOW THE COUNTRY CODE

Enjoy the countryside and respect its life and work

Guard against all risk of fire

Fasten all gates

Keep your dogs under close control

Keep to public paths across farmland

Leave livestock, crops and machinery alone

Use gates and stiles to cross fences, hedges and walls

Take your litter home

Help to keep all water clean

Protect wildlife, plants and trees

Take special care on country roads

Make no unnecessary noise

Reproduced by permission of the Countryside Commission

1 Twm Siôn Catti's Cave

Start:	RSPB car park, Dinas Nature Reserve, 1 mile (1.5 km) south of Llyn Brianne Reservoir
Distance:	2½ miles (4 km)
Approximate time:	1½ hours
Parking:	RSPB car park
Refreshments:	None
Ordnance Survey maps:	Landrangers 146 (Lampeter & Llandovery) or 147 (Elan Valley & Builth Wells), Pathfinder 1013, SN 64/74 (Cilycwm & Pumsaint)

General description *This is classified as an easy walk because the circular, way-marked RSPB Nature Reserve route is essentially that. However, the diversion up to Twm Siôn Catti's Cave is strenuous, so please treat this ¼ mile (0.5 km) as an optional extension. An elevated board-walk carries walkers over the marshy ground between car park and wooded hill. A shady path then leads around the hill, with exciting views over a dramatic river for half the way. The keen and hardy will*

enjoy the bonus of the climb to the famous cave. If you must bring a dog, do ensure that you keep it under control in this wildlife reserve.

If you are lucky, you may see a red kite in the sky. They survived here when facing extinction. Ironically, now their numbers are increasing, none nests at Dinas. You may see buzzards, peregrines, kestrels and sparrow-hawks. Tree-pipits and red-starts frequent the open areas, while pied flycatchers enjoy the shelter of the oak woodland. Look out too for wood-warblers, woodpeckers, nuthatches and tree-creepers.

Take the kissing-gate in the bottom left corner of the car park. Walk on the raised boardwalk, with a stream on your right. This boardwalk allows views of marsh marigolds, orchids and golden saxifrage, with damselflies and dragonflies in the air. Dippers and common sandpipers visit the steams and rivers. Goosanders with their chicks are a feature of June. Enter broadleaved woodland and reach a T-junction, waymarked by a white boot-print (**A**). The boardwalk has now ended.

Bear left to circle round the wooded hill on your right. The perimeter fence of the woodland is on your left, and there is a road below on the left and bare pasture across the valley. Notice a disused quarry high up on the slope away to your left. Continue along the clear path around the hillside to come to an attractive river on your left. The confluence of the Doethie and Towy rivers precedes dramatic cataracts in the Afon Tywi (River Towy). The path makes a hairpin bend and climbs steps so that you are soon walking above the river on your left again. Reach a viewpoint with a bench at waymark post No. 4 (**B**).

If you feel up to the steep ascent, divert right here along the rough path up the hillside. The scramble is worth it when you reach the cave. Surrounded by trees and boulders, it is necessary to get down on hands and knees to crawl into this. Part of the roof has fallen in, making it now a crevice rather than a cave. You will know you are in the right place by the initials and dates carved on the rock inside. One date reads '1832' (**C**).

Born around 1530, Twm Siôn Catti became as famous in Wales as Robin Hood in England. His mother was Catti Jones of Tregaron, who named him Thomas John, hence Twm Siôn. Being illegitimate, he added his mother's name rather than the surname of his father, Siôn ap Dafydd ap Madog ap Hywel Moetheu of Porth-y-ffin, near Tregaron.

The elevated boardwalk at the start of the route to Twm Siôn Catti's Cave

Twm became an impudent, cunning rogue. His career may have been a means of survival during the reign of Queen Mary, when his preference for the Protestant religion made him a rebel. He fled to Geneva in 1550. The accession of Queen Elizabeth brought him an official pardon in 1559. It did not mention the nature of his crime, but apocryphal tales are legion. They were recorded in 1828 by T.J. Llewelyn Pritchard in *The Adventures and Vagaries of Twm Shon Catti*, which portrayed him as a popular hero who robbed the rich to give to the poor.

Twm was not averse to a spot of highway robbery, so long as his victims were rich. One day he held up a squire and his lovely daughter. Twm fell in love with her and returned her jewellery. He then campaigned to marry her, against her father's opposition; he had, after all, been robbed of his cash. This cave made a convenient base for him, being not too far from her home, whilst providing refuge from pursuers. One full moon he crept to her window and caught her outstretched hand and kissed it. He refused to let it go until she promised to marry him. When she would not agree, he drew blood with his blade and threatened to cut the hand off. This quickly brought the required promise from the girl, who really did marry him. She was actually the widow of the Sheriff of Carmarthen, and Twm soon obtained a general pardon and respectable status in society. Appointed a Justice of the Peace, he held this position until his death in 1609.

Retrace your steps to waymark post No. 4 at the viewpoint and resume walking with the river below on your left. The path eventually bears right from the river to take you back to the T-junction at the head of the boardwalk. Turn left to retrace your steps along this, back to the car park. □

2 Llanddewi-Brefi

Start:	Llanddewi-Brefi
Distance:	2¹⁄₂ miles (4 km)
approximate time:	1¹⁄₂ hours
Parking:	Llanddewi-Brefi, near the church
Refreshments:	Pub at Llanddewi-Brefi
Ordnance Survey: maps:	Landranger 146 (Lampeter & Llandovery), Pathfinder 990, SN 65/75 (Tregaron & Llanddewi-Brefi)

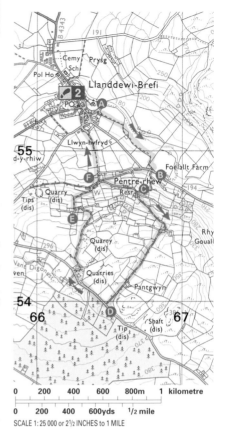

SCALE 1:25 000 or 2¹⁄₂ INCHES to 1 MILE

General description *Good tracks make the climbing easy on this short walk. Allow time to visit the church, which is one of the most sacred spots in Wales. The route climbs to the south of the village to enjoy glorious views up the Teifi valley towards Tregaron, and the church guides pilgrims on the way back down.*

Start from the church at Llanddewi-Brefi (**A**). In the sixth century this was the scene of an important ecclesiastical convocation. Its purpose was, according to legend, to deal with the Pelagian heresy. Academics have disputed this, suggesting that a synod was held to draw up a code of discipline for clergy and laity.

Pelagius was an Ulsterman who travelled to Rome and spoke in favour of salvation by deeds, based on free will, rather than relying on divine grace. He also, it seems, believed in reincarnation. The Church, now basking in its status as the official religion of the Roman Empire, could no longer tolerate such ideas. Pelagius – which was the Latinised version of his Celtic name Morgan, meaning 'born over the sea' – was condemned as a heretic in AD 418. His ideas remained well rooted in this part of Wales, however. When the synod was called to tackle the problem, a great multitude converged here, and the noise was such that nobody could be heard. St David had chosen to stay away, but reluctantly came at the request of the assembled clerics. He spoke clearly and convincingly in favour of the doctrine of divine grace. The argument was settled by the miracle of the ground rising beneath St David's feet so that he could be seen and heard by the throng. Also, a white dove settled on his shoulder. The church was built on the raised mound and houses ancient tombstones, including one dating from

the early seventh century and deciphered as: *Hic iacet Idnert, filius Jacobi qui occisus fuit propter predam santi david* 'Here lies Idnert, son of Jacob who was killed as a result of the plunder of David's sanctuary'. This seems to be the earliest written reference to Wales' patron saint. Other stones have both Latin and Ogham inscriptions, while there is a modern statue of St David. A college made the village a seat of learning throughout the Dark and Middle Ages. The library of Jesus College, Oxford, now houses *The Book of the Anchorite*, compiled in Llanddewi-Brefi in 1346. This gives the final message of St David to his followers just before he died, in 589, as: 'Lords, brothers and sisters, be happy and keep your faith and your belief, and do the little things that you have heard and seen me do.' How typical of David that emphasis should be on the 'little things', the apparently trivial acts of kindness and self-forgetfulness that are so essential to generate a sense of community.

The sacred nature of this place is much older than St David. It is associated with Hu Gadarn 'Huw the Mighty', who led the

Cymri to Britain from present-day Turkey nearly 4,000 years ago. His standard was an ox, being the origin of the sobriquet 'John Bull', perhaps a reference to the Age of Taurus. The personification of intellectual culture, he made poetry the vehicle of the memory and invented the Triads. Ogham characters, glass-making and much else were attributed to him. Hu is also associated with the last two long-horned oxen *ychen bannog*. While pulling a great stone to build the church at Llanddewi-Brefi, they made a *cwys* 'furrow' on the mountain known as Cwys-yr-Ychen-bannog, 3 miles (4.75 km) north-east of Tregaron. The effort killed one of the oxen and its partner then bellowed nine times to split open a rock in the way of the stone they were hauling, before it, too, died. The root *bref-* in the place-name refers to these bellows:

Speckled Llanddewi-Brefi
Where the ox bellowed nine times
Until it split open the Foelallt Rock.

An ox horn used to be kept in the church at Llanddewi-Brefi, giving substance to this legend.

With your back to the church, go left along the road and fork left, as signed for a youth hostel. Soon fork left again up a 'no through road'. Bear right at the next fork to follow a track that is signposted as public footpath. After passing cottages on your right, enter a field and go ahead with a fence on the right. Continue through a kissing-gate in the corner, cross a ditch and turn right to walk along the right-hand edge of a meadow. Bear right in its far corner to follow a path that turns left over a stile beside a gate to climb to a road. You reach the road (**B**) near Foelallt Farm, with the rock split by the bellowing ox,

Craig y Foelallt, behind you, across the valley of the River Brefi.

Turn right along the road and bear left when you come to a fork. This rough lane passes cottages on the left, including one with the legend 'David Daniel built this house in 1758'. Bear right to pass a house on the right (**C**) and follow an old green lane. Climb with a wall and a view across the valley to Craig y Foelallt on the left. Ignore a descending track on the left. Reach an isolated farmhouse and turn sharply right, then bear left uphill with a track coming from your right. Emerge on a lane opposite a conifer forest (**D**).

Turn right down the lane. Notice when the conifers give way to pasture on the left, then pass a belt of trees and go ahead about 30 yards (27 m) before turning sharply right. This track climbs to a junction near old, disused quarries on the right. Turn left to walk along a fenced track past more disused quarries on the right and gradually downhill. The great bog north of Tregaron can be seen ahead.

Pass a farmhouse on the left and (**E**) turn right down a narrow path. Reach a broader, walled path and bear right down to the track junction visited on your outward route. Ignore a path descending on the left. The right of way continues past a cottage on the right.

Go slightly left at the track junction (**F**) to bear right down a woodland path. Go ahead through a small gate and walk with a wall on the right. Continue through a kissing-gate in the corner and go across the middle of this field, heading for the church tower. Continue through a kissing-gate in the wall ahead. A shady path leads to the football pitch, on the left, and the village, ahead. Bear right and fork left to return to the start of this walk. ☐

A view from the route, overlooking Llanddewi-Brefi and the Teifi valley

3 Leominster

Start:	Leominster
Distance:	3 miles (4.75 km)
Approximate time:	1½ hours
Parking:	Leominster
Refreshments:	Pubs and cafés at Leominster
Ordnance Survey maps:	Landranger 149 (Hereford & Leominster) Pathfinder 994, SO 45/55 (Leominster)

General description *Leominster, pronounced 'Lemster', occupies a strategic position near the border of England and Wales. This has made it vulnerable to attack in the past but now adds a special flavour to this walk. The route passes Leominster Station in both directions, then follows a path beside the River Lugg, crosses meadows and gradually climbs the slope of Eaton Hill for a view over the town. Allow time if you wish to visit the ancient Priory Church before completing the walk, and don't miss visiting the town.*

Starting at the excellent tourist information centre at one corner of Corn Square,

go towards Lloyds Bank at the end of this square and take the path ahead that passes Lloyds Bank on your left. This is Grange Walk. It leads to the car park, on your right, while passing the cricket pitch on your left. Grange Court is the black and white timber-framed building ahead on your left. Continue with the iron railings of its garden fence on the left and a fence then a wall on the right.

Soon fork right between red-brick walls to Falconer Place. Go right to join Etnam Street and turn left along its pavement to reach the White Lion Inn (**A**). The railway station is nearby, about 150 yards (137 m) along Worcester Road, on your right.

Leaving Worcester Road on your right, go ahead along the signposted public footpath that passes the garden of the White Lion Inn on your left. Cross a footbridge over the railway. Go ahead to cross a bridge over the River Lugg (**B**). This river is bordered by Lammas Meadows, which are open for communal grazing at the start of August. These give a clue to the river's name because Lammas was the Celtic festival of Lugnasadh (1 August).

Turn left along the signposted footpath, which begins by going down a flight of steps. Walk with the river on your left along the left-hand edge of a meadow. This still floods regularly in winter, with the silt deposited by the receding waters

Grange Court, Leominster

fertilising the soil and building up a level surface. Underlying gravel gives good drainage, so the meadow does not become water-logged.

Reach a public footpath signpost near a stile. Cross the latter to bear right, as signposted, away from the flat, concrete bridge over the river on your left. Come to the A49 road and cross it carefully. Go ahead through a kissing-gate and follow the signposted path. Walk along a firm track beside a hedge on your left and an arable field on your right. The new A49, Leominster bypass, runs on a causeway to avoid the floods and bisects the former meadow, which has resulted in the eastern part becoming arable land.

Go ahead through gates at the foot of the slope of Eaton Hill (**C**). Bear right, as waymarked, to climb uphill. At the crest of Eaton Hill, go right to walk along the ridge, as waymarked, with a fence on your left and a view over the town and valley on your right.

Continue over a waymarked stile with a patch of woodland obscuring the view on your right (**D**). Emerge over a second stile to walk with a hedge on the right and a field on the left. The path turns into an old hollow way as it gradually bears right, downhill.

Cross a waymarked stile at a path junction (**E**) and fork right downhill. Reach a waymark post and take a gap in the lower hedge, graced by an old, stone staircase. Emerge into a lower field and bear right, as waymarked, to descend with a hedge on your right. A stile ahead at the foot of this field gives access to the A44. Turn right along its pavement. Pass Westeaton House, a residential home for the elderly, on your right. Notice a lane signposted for Stoke Prior on the left. Bear right here (**F**) to cross a stile and take the signposted path diagonally across a meadow to the River Lugg.

Reach the river about 150 yards (137 m) from the road bridge on the left, known as Lugg Bridge. Turn right to walk with the river on your left. Continue under the new A49 road bridge. Go up steps in the corner of the next field to retrace your steps across the bridge taken on your outward journey. Cross the railway bridge and emerge past the garden of the White Lion Inn on the right. The railway station is along Worcester Road on your left. This route continues with Etnam Street towards the town centre.

Retrace your steps through Falconer Place to Grange Court. Divert along the path going right to the magnificent old Priory Church, originally part of an eleventh-century monastery. It contains the last used ducking-stool in England, dating from 1809. Return to Corn Square, where the tourist information centre has copies of an interesting Town Trail. □

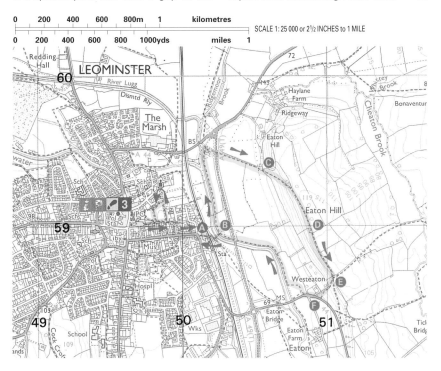

SCALE 1:25 000 or 2½ INCHES to 1 MILE

4 Llanwrtyd Wells

Start:	Llanwrtyd Wells
Distance:	3½ miles (5.5 km)
Approximate time:	2 hours
Parking:	Llanwrtyd Wells
Refreshments:	Tearoom and pubs at Llanwrtyd Wells
Ordnance Survey maps:	Landranger 147 (Elan Valley & Builth Wells), Pathfinder 1014, SN 84/94 (Llanwrtyd Wells)

General description *This is a stroll through the smallest town in Britain and up the valley of the River Irfon to the old church at Llanwrtyd Without. One of Wales' greatest hymn writers used to serve as a curate here. The route returns down the other side of the valley, along quiet lanes and riverside paths, passing a hotel where people used to stay when taking the water at this former spa.*

With a population of about 600, Llanwrtyd Wells (**A**) rejoices in the title of Britain's smallest town. It has a station on the scenic Heart of Wales railway line, linking Swansea with Shrewsbury, and this walk starts from the station.

Go left along Station Road and turn left across the bridge to reach the Calvinistic Methodist chapel on the eastern side of the bridge and pass the signed car park on the right. Cars are best parked here in the centre of town.

Turn right up Victoria Road, which is a 'no through road'. Bear right at a fork (**B**) to take a shady lane past a meadow on your right. The lane becomes a riverside path after passing Dol-gau. Walk upstream with the River Irfon on your right, ignoring a footbridge across it. Step over a tributary stream and emerge from trees to bear left across the corner of a field to a gate on your right in the top corner. Go ahead through it and across a stream to join a lane on the left, near the Victoria Wells Chalet Motel (**C**). Victoria Wells Spa was opened in 1897, when Queen Victoria celebrated her Jubilee.

Go ahead along the lane, passing the motel on your left. Notice another footbridge across the river, below on your right. Reach a junction with the track that descends to it but ignore this by going straight ahead through a gate to follow a grass track. This leads to the river on your right before bearing left to join a rough, firm lane, which you turn right along. Pass Dinas Mill on the left and reach St David's Church, Llanwrtyd Without (**D**).

This ancient church was founded by St David himself in the sixth century. Its

St David's Church, Llanwrtyd Without

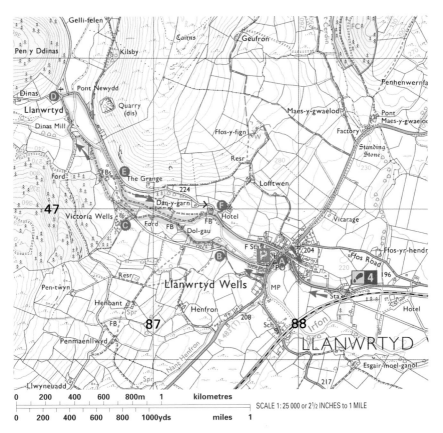

vicar from 1732 to 1767 was Theophilus Evans, who first discovered the health spring that was to make the town such a popular spa in the nineteenth century, especially after the coming of the railway in 1867. Theophilus Evans' curate from 1740 to 1743 was William Williams, who lived in his old home at Pantycelyn whilst being responsible for this parish.

Educated to be a doctor, William Williams became a convert to Methodism after hearing Hywel Harris preach in 1738. He and Theophilus Evans could not agree about Methodism, so he was expelled from the Church in 1743. The people of Llanwrtyd signed a petition supporting his expulsion from the living, so he became a travelling preacher. His travels inspired him to become a great hymn-writer, with 'Guide Me, O Thou Great Jehovah' his best-known hymn.

Two composers are buried in the graveyard: John Thomas 'Llanwrtyd' (1839–1921) and D.C. 'Christmas' Williams (1871–1926). Look, too, for the tomb of James Rhys 'Kilsby' Jones (1813–89). Amongst many other things, he campaigned against the Welsh language, persuading Parliament to send commissioners to Wales to investigate education in 1847. This led to the 'Treachery of the Blue Books'.

Take the road down from the church to cross a bridge over the River Irfon. Go down the valley, with the river on your right. When the road starts to climb and bear left, away from the river, fork right (**E**). Follow the signposted path with the river on your right, ignoring footbridges across it. Reach the disused Dol-y-Coed Hotel (**F**), which is passed on the left.

Dol-y-Coed Hotel played an important part in the development of the spa town. Formerly a country-house, the original Ffynnon Drewllyd 'Stinking Well' was found in its grounds by Theophilus Evans in 1732. Suffering from scurvy, he was desperate enough to taste the water, but only after a little frog has seemed to invite him to do so. Most of the buildings date from 1884, but the Rhys Jones family was forced to sell their investment in 1934. The spa has been disused since the late 1950s.

Bear right along a road back into the centre of Llanwrtyd Wells. Turn right across the bridge to return to the car park, or go ahead along Station Road to return to the station.   □

5 Castle Caereinion

Start: Castle Caereinion Station

Distance: 3½ miles (5.5 km)

Approximate time: 2 hours

Parking: Castle Caereinion Station

Refreshments: Pub and shop at Castle Caereinion

Ordnance Survey maps: Landranger 125 (Bala & Lake Vyrnwy), Pathfinder 887, SJ 00/01 (Llanfair Caereinion)

General description *Castle Caereinion's station comes between Welshpool and Llanfair Caereinion on the delightful Welshpool & Llanfair Light Railway. The walk follows the road from the station to the historic village and then westwards along a hedged track, around a wooded dingle and across pasture to woodland that shelters ponds. Fieldpaths that lead through forest offer admirable views before rejoining the old lane on the return journey. Much of this route follows permissive paths. The steam train service to Castle Caereinion (Tel: 01938 810441) is seasonal, so check the timetable before setting out. Trains run from Llanfair Caereinion and Welshpool. Both places have car parks and can be reached by bus.*

Go left from the station and up the B4385 road to the edge of Castle Caereinion, where you turn right along a firm, hedged track, Henrhyd Lane. After 300 yards (274 m), turn right through a small wooden gate to descend with woodland on your left and a fence on your right. Cross a footbridge over a stream in the bottom of the dingle and bear left uphill, keeping just inside the woodland. Descend to take a second footbridge (**A**). Bear right, climbing to a perimeter fence near sheep-pens.

Now that the dingle is fenced off, cattle and sheep no longer use it for shelter. Beech, oak, cherry and sycamore trees are thriving, while May is the month to admire the bluebells. This route goes right, along the rim of the wooded dingle, until a stile invites you to bear left across the long, narrow field to a stile beside a gate in its top corner.

Go right up the firm track of Henrhyd Lane, soon passing Henrhyd Cottage on your right. Its name means 'old ford', and it is much easier to cross the stream here than in the steeply sided dingle. Follow the track through a gate and bear left, as waymarked, through an oak and beech copse (**B**). Continue over open pasture when the track ends. At first there is a fence on your right. When this turns right, go straight ahead to an isolated oak tree and just beyond it cross a stile beside a metal gate in the perimeter fence of some woodland.

Continue ahead along a grassy path for

SCALE 1:25 000 or 2½ INCHES to 1 MILE

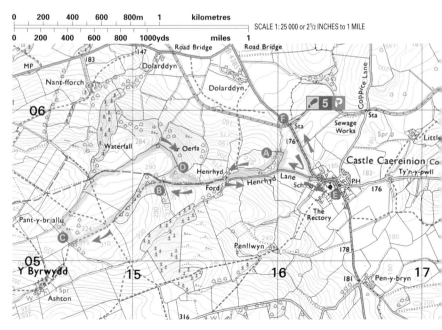

Castle Caereinion Station

10 yards (9 m) then fork right along a narrower woodland path. Pass a pond **(C)** on your left and turn left, as waymarked, to take a causeway between this and a second pond. These artificial ponds provide an emergency water supply for cattle as well as habitats for wildlife. They are surrounded by oak, willow and hazel trees, as well as some conifers. Bear right to take a narrow path between the trees and emerge over a waymarked stile in a fence ahead, which is near a corner on your left.

Bear slightly left through low woodland to cross a footbridge over the course of a seasonal stream. Continue over a stile in the fence ahead. Walk above a wooded slope on your left, keeping to the left-hand edge of open, upland pasture on Y Byrwydd. Go ahead over another stile. Keep beside the hedge on your left as it swings right. Eventually, reach a corner where a waymarked stile directs you into a larch plantation **(D)**.

Bear right with the established path through this portion of forest, turn left downhill with it and go left along the foot of the slope, with trees on your left and a fence on your right. When a fence appears ahead, turn right to cross a small footbridge over a ditch and take a stile to reach open pasture. Go ahead, as waymarked, to rejoin the firm track of Henrhyd Lane.

Go left down the lane back to the outskirts of Castle Caereinion. Turn right if you wish to divert into the village, which has a shop opposite the Red Lion pub.

This ancient settlement was named after the fort of Einion Yrth, who was the local lord who ruled from AD 389 to 443. A twelfth-century castle built by Madog ap Maredudd, prince of Powys, can be traced in the churchyard of St Garmon's **(E)**. This church is named after the French bishop who came to Wales in AD 429 to suppress the Pelagian heresy being promoted by an Ulsterman who believed in reincarnation and the law of cause and effect, rather than original sin.

Retrace your steps down the road to the railway station. The railway **(F)** arrived here in 1903 with a gauge of 2 feet 6 inches (0.76 m). It benefited from the Light Railways Act of 1896 that allowed rural lines to be constructed without costly, specific Acts of Parliament. Cheaper to build, such railways were nevertheless subject to speed and weight restrictions. Mainly an agricultural line, it carried large quantities of timber during the First World War. The Great Western Railway took the line over in 1923 and axed passenger services in 1931, in favour of their quicker bus service from Welshpool to Dinas Mawddwy via Llanfair. The last goods train ran in 1956, but by 1963 enthusiasts had reopened the line from Llanfair Caereinion for passengers. Raven Square, Welshpool, was reached in 1981 and has become the eastern terminus. Gone for ever is the stretch on Welshpool's streets to the town's station on the Shrewsbury–Aberystwyth line. The railway's exotic passenger stock includes coaches from Sierra Leone and Austria. □

6 Kington

Start:	Kington
Distance:	3½ miles (5.5 km)
Approximate time:	2 hours
Parking:	Kington
Refreshments:	Pubs and cafés at Kington
Ordnance Survey maps:	Landranger 148 (Presteigne & Hay-on-Wye), Pathfinder 993, SO 25/35 (Kington)

General description *It is easy to follow this route as it winds through a typical Marches town, complete with historical characters, an old tramway, a toll-house and, of course, a clock tower. The Offa's Dyke Path is followed past the gardens of the botanical Banks family, which are open from April to October, and a firm track affords views over the valley of the River Arrow and Hergest Court. The return to the centre of the town is along grassy paths past blackberry bushes and sports pitches.*

Start from Kington's tourist information centre, near which is a car park. There is a museum across the road. Go right to pass this on your left and reach the clock tower (**A**) on the left. Turn left up Church Street.

This busy little market town may have earned its name shortly before 1066, when Harold Godwinson established firm English rule here because the town appeared vulnerable to Welsh claims. Welsh drovers continued to invade the place, however, until the opening of the railway from Leominster in 1857 made their services redundant. One old drover, named Stafford, used to sleep in a broken tomb in the churchyard. Calling from his 'bed' in the mornings, he frightened many passers-by.

Another character who graced Kington was the actress Sarah Siddons. Born in Brecon in 1755, she made her stage debut in this town. Her final performance, in 1812, was at Covent Garden as Lady Macbeth, when the audience forced the play to end, with tears all round, after her last scene. Her brother, Stephen Kemble, was also an actor connected with Kington.

Turn right at the war memorial, near the Swan Hotel. Go to the end of The Square and take the road that leads from its left-hand corner to another square. Leave this at its top right-hand corner to take a lane that soon bears left downhill. Go ahead at a crossroads down a 'no through road' called Crooked Well. William Wordsworth once lived down here. Bear left with the lane to walk with a stream on your right. A footbridge on the right has an acorn symbol on it to show that the Offa's Dyke Path passes over it (**B**). Your way lies ahead, keeping the stream on the right.

Continue along a narrow path above the stream, on the right. Diverge from the stream to pass a green space populated by geese on the right and reach a sign-posted path junction. Turn right through a kissing-gate to continue with a fence on the right along the route of the old tramway.

The tramway was a forerunner of the railway in an age when canals were seen as the way to transport heavy, bulky goods such as coal. The expense of digging canals demanded a large amount of traffic to justify it. In the eighteenth century, horses were found to be able to haul heavier loads when their carts ran along special iron tracks, rather than on the pot-holed roads. These tramways fed into the canal system. The canal from Abergavenny to Brecon was extended by a tramway from Brecon to Hay-on-Wye and on to Eardisley by 1818. It reached Kington in 1820 and finished at the limestone quarries at Burlingjobb, near Old Radnor and New Radnor.

The rails were not like those of modern railways. They were made in L-shaped sections to contain the flat wheels of the trucks, rather than modern railway flanged wheels. The gauge was 3 feet 6 inches (1.05 m). Coal and iron were brought cheaply from South Wales, and a foundry was built at Kington. Lime was taken down the line in exchange, along with agricultural produce.

The path swings right to put the stream on the right again. Pass another footbridge across it, then turn sharply left uphill to reach a lane. Turn right and bear left when the lane ends at a fork of two paths. Emerge at a road and go left along it for 20 yards (18 m) to a turning on the right, which is a 'no through road' (**C**).

Turn right along the causewayed pavement of this 'no through road', which is Ridgebourne Road and part of the Offa's Dyke Path. It leads past Hergest Croft Gardens on the left. Open daily on afternoons from April to October, this fine collection of trees and shrubs includes delightful spring and summer borders and a kitchen garden. Rhododendrons grow tall in a hidden valley.

Look for a roughly surfaced lane on the left and turn left down it to reach Haywood Farm (**D**). Keep descending with the

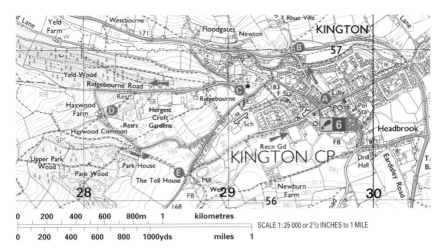

lane, which is revealed as Cutterbach Lane when it joins a road. Turn right along the road to reach a signposted public footpath on the left, which turns sharply back towards Kington (**E**). If you were to continue along this road a few more paces, you would come to the old toll-house. In the 1830s, this part of Herefordshire was visited by the Daughters of Rebecca, determined to 'possess the gates of them that hate them'. Men dressed as women burnt down the hated toll-gates at night.

Just 1 mile (1.5 km) down the road is Hergest Court, the seat of the Vaughans during the Middle Ages. This was where the Red and White Books of Hergest were kept. *The Red Book of Hergest* has survived and is in the Bodleian Library, Oxford. Much of *The Mabinogion* is based on it.

Hergest Court was also the home of Thomas (Black) Vaughan, who was killed in the Battle of Banbury during the Wars

of the Roses in 1469. His ghost returned to this area and had to be exorcised. His spirit was put in a silver snuff-box and left at the bottom of Hergest Pool. One day the pool was drained and the spirit released from the snuff-box. Old Vaughan is said to appear regularly in the form of a supernatural black dog, which may have inspired Conan Doyle to write *The Hound of the Baskervilles*.

Take the signposted path back towards Kington, passing a garden wall on your left and a hedge on the right. Go ahead through a kissing-gate and along the left-hand edge of a field. Continue through another kissing-gate to walk with the hedge now on your right. Cross school playing-fields and enter the recreation ground. Take a gate from this to maintain your direction along Park Avenue, which becomes Mill Street. This leads back to the car park and tourist information centre on the right. □

Skirting Haywood Common, west of Kington

7 Llanidloes

Start:	Llanidloes
Distance:	3½ miles (5.5 km)
Approximate time:	2 hours
Parking:	Llandiloes
Refreshments:	Cafés and pubs at Llanidloes
Ordnance Survey maps:	Landranger 136 (Newtown & Llanidloes), Pathfinder 928, SN 88/98 (Llanidloes)

General description *A moderately steep descent through woodland makes this otherwise easy walk somewhat more demanding. It climbs with a track from Llanidloes and continues along field paths, taking in the view from a plateau, before descending the wooded slope to a path that overlooks the River Clywedog. The route then accompanies the river down its valley to return to the historic town of Llanidloes.*

The entrance to the riverside car park and bus station at Llanidloes is opposite the Mount Inn. Facing this pub, turn left into the centre of Llanidloes, where the half-timbered Market Hall has survived since around 1600 (**A**). Now a museum, it has seen stirring times. The town was a major centre for weaving in the early nineteenth century, but the wages were low and the harvests were poor. With the French Revolution still in the minds of many, not least the authorities, matters came to a head in Llanidloes between 30 April and 4 May 1839.

Chartists were active here, either encouraging or responding to the discontented workers. This movement took its name from the People's Charter of 1838. This demanded votes for all men, equal electoral districts, vote by secret ballot, annually elected parliaments, the payment of MPs and the abolition of property qualifications for membership. Many advocated peaceful reform, based on 'moral force', but some extremists were prepared for violence. A chief focus of hatred was the newly built workhouse at Caersws – now a hospital, passed on Walk 11. The Poor Law Act of 1834 had replaced poor-relief with workhouses. Wages were low and working conditions bad. Rents were high, and the workers were crowded into insanitary living accommodation. Not surprisingly, interest in Chartism was strong.

A public meeting was held early in 1839 at which a Chartist leader, Hetherington, from London, spoke about the Charter. He later promoted the stock-piling of firearms at a private meeting with the leading Llanidloes Chartists. The younger ones were easily swayed and 'borrowed' guns from local farmers. One home-made

The Market Hall, Llanidloes

dagger was found when the authorities investigated.

T.E. Marsh, a local landowner and former mayor, determined to stamp out the perceived threat to his interests. He enlisted his tenants as 'special' constables, while three constables arrived from London. The next morning, 30 April, saw a confrontation between the weavers and the 'specials' when news came that three Chartist leaders had been arrested. The weavers, some with guns, managed to release them, whilst badly beating up one of the London policemen.

Moderate Chartists managed to quieten the mob, but Marsh rode to the Lord Lieutenant to ask for troops to quell the rioters. They marched at break-neck speed from Brecon and arrived on the morning of 4 May. They were relieved to find their services were not required. Marsh seems to have influenced the magistrates, however. The town was sealed off on 6 May and thirty-two arrests were made. Despite the doubtful evidence, thirty were convicted, with sentences ranging between two months' hard labour and fifteen years' transportation to Australia.

Turn left along Short Bridge Street and go ahead across the bridge over the River Severn. Turn right, then immediately left and follow a rough track through a gate (**B**). Continue climbing and overlook Llanidloes on your left. Ignore side-tracks on the right, while the main track swings gradually right. When the firm track bears left towards Penybanc (**C**), go straight ahead along the right-hand edge of a field. Continue through a corner of woodland to cross wooden bars which serve as a stile. Maintain your direction, passing a gate in the corner of the field on your right. Go ahead across high pasture.

Go through a gate in a fence ahead and continue beside a fence on the right, soon ignoring a gate in it. Descend to a junction of farm tracks (**D**). Turn right through a double metal field gate and follow a track across two fields towards a forest. Take a wooden gate into this forest and go up along a forest track for 100 yards (91 m) (**E**).

Bear left into the forest and descend to a track running along the foot of its slope. Go right along this track, with the forest on the right and the River Clywedog below sloping meadows on the left. Take the lower track at a fork and continue across a stile, just below a gate marked 'private' (**F**).

Go ahead along the top of a sloping meadow. On the opposite bank of the river, away to your left, is a caravan park. Go ahead through a kissing-gate in the corner, followed by a footbridge. Climb the next field to a stile behind a tree. Bear left along a lane. Go ahead along this, keeping above the river on your left and heading towards Llanidloes. Ignore lanes on the right. Descend to the bridge over the River Severn and turn left to retrace your steps into the town. □

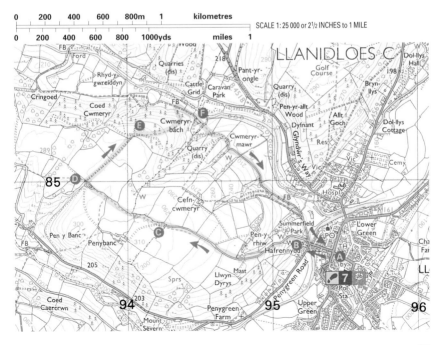

SCALE 1:25 000 or 2½ INCHES to 1 MILE

8 Aberedw

Start:	Aberedw
Distance:	4 miles (6.5 km)
Approximate time:	2 hours
Parking:	Aberedw, near the church and pub
Refreshments:	Pub at Aberedw
Ordnance Survey maps:	Landranger 147 (Elan Valley & Builth Wells), Pathfinder 1015, SO 04/14 (Aberedw)

General description *There is a hill to climb on this route, but there is a good track up it at a gentle gradient, so this counts as an easy walk. Having gained the height, enjoy the view across the Wye valley into the Eppynt and south to the Brecon Beacons. The route then returns along the lane into the village of Aberedw, with its attractive old church and pub.*

Face the Seven Sisters Inn at Aberedw and go left down the lane, passing the old church (**A**) on your right. Two large yew trees betray the great age of this sacred spot. The church is dedicated to

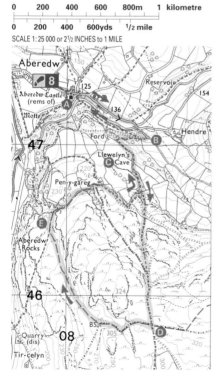

SCALE 1: 25 000 or 2½ INCHES to 1 MILE

St Cwydd, a brother of Gildas, who lived in the sixth century. Admire the unusual porch, made from mighty oak beams.

Fork right to pass a telephone-box on your left and walk above the River Edw on the right. Descend with the lane to a stone bridge and cross the river by it. Bear right at a fork to climb uphill for about 100 yards (91 m).

Turn sharply right to go through a gate (**B**) and follow a rough track that climbs gradually. Bear left with it at the top of the wooded slope. Go through a gate and walk with a hedge on your right. Pass a gate on your right. This gives access to Llywelyn's Cave (**C**), which is in woodland on the left-hand side of the field. However, there is no right of way to it. Prince Llywelyn the Last spent his last night alive here in December 1282. The next morning he determined to seek shelter from the pursuing English in the castle at nearby Builth. Legend has it that he tried to confuse the enemy by having the shoes of his horse reversed so that his tracks might suggest he was moving in the opposite direction. In the event, John Gifford, the governor of Builth Castle, refused Llywelyn shelter. The English soon captured the prince, killed and beheaded him, and sent his head to Edward I as a trophy for display at the Tower of London.

Continuing along the main track, pass a farm on your right and reach a junction.

The Wye valley from Aberedw Rocks

Ignore the firm track bearing right. Go ahead along a clear grass track. Continue across a firm track, keeping to the grass one running ahead through the bracken. Bear left to maintain your direction when another path converges with yours, coming sharply from the right. Take the left of two paths going ahead across the plateau. Go straight ahead at the first crosstracks, where the track on the right leads to a pond nestling at the foot of crags.

Turn right at the second crosstracks (**D**). Gradually descend with the track below the crags on your right. Depart from the grass track that bears left through the bracken by forking right along a path that passes below the crags about 100 yards (91 m) away on the right. Bear right at a fork. Eventually, emerge from the bracken at the foot of Aberedw Rocks, on your right (**E**).

Continue past a rocky hollow on the left, pass a field gate on the left and walk with a fence on the left and a bracken-covered slope ascending on the right. When the fence turns left, bear left uphill above it and reach an abandoned farmhouse. Turn right, away from this. Bear left at a fork to take the track down to the farmhouse passed on the outward journey and go left downhill to retrace your steps to Aberedw.

The Reverend Francis Kilvert came this way on Tuesday, 13 April 1875. Recording his thoughts in the diary that was to make him famous, he wrote:

'Oh, Aberedw, Aberedw. Would God I might dwell and die by thee. Memory enters in and brings back the old time in a clear vision and waking dream, and again I descend from the high moor's half encircling sweep and listen to the distant murmur of the river as it foams down the ravine from its home in the Green Cwm and its cradle in the hills. Once more I stand by the riverside and look up at the cliff castle towers and mark the wild roses swinging from the crag and watch the green woods waving and shimmering with a twinkling dazzle as they rustle in the breeze and shining of the summer afternoon, while here and there a grey crag peeps from among the tufted trees. And once again I hear the merry voices and laughter of the children as they clamber down the cliff path among the bushes or along the rock ledges of the riverside or climb the Castle Mount, or saunter along the narrow green meadow tree-fringed and rock-bordered and pass in and out of Llewellyn's cave, or gather wood and light the fire amongst the rocks upon the moor, or loiter down the valley to Cavan Twm Bach and cross the shining ferry at sunset, when the evening shadows lie long and still across the broad reaches of the river. Oh, Aberedw, Aberedw.' ☐

9 Aberystwyth

Start:	Aberystwyth
Distance:	4 miles (6.5 km)
Approximate time:	2 hours
Parking:	Aberystwyth
Refreshments:	Pubs and cafés at Aberystwyth
Ordnance Survey maps:	Landranger 135 (Aberystwyth), Pathfinder 926, SN 57/58 (Aberystwyth)

General description *Visitors to 'Aber' are surprised to find that the town is situated on the River Rheidol, rather than the Ystwyth. This walk takes you to the original hilltop settlement, now crowned by a monument to the Duke of Welling-ton, and does, indeed, overlook the River Ystwyth. See a model of the hillfort in the Ceredigion Museum, near the end of this walk.*

Aberystwyth exchanges its population of university students for an influx of holidaymakers each summer, bringing a constant vibrant pulse to the unofficial capital of West Wales. Some say the nation's capital should be here, as it is in a cultural sense, with the impressive National Library of Wales on the hillside just below the University College of Wales. This walk will show you how such facilities are contained in a town too small to suffer from the drawbacks of urban life, with ready access to beautiful country-side.

The railway station is built like a grand terminus. Trains arrive here from Birmingham and Shrewsbury, while this is also the place to take the steam train up the Vale of Rheidol to Devil's Bridge. The bus-stops are outside the station, while one of several car parks is just around the corner, in Park Avenue. With your back to the front of the station, facing the row of telephone-boxes, go right and turn right (**A**) through the gates of Plascrug Avenue.

Pass a children's playground on your right and notice the classical building of

SCALE 1:25 000 or 2½ INCHES to 1 MILE

Looking across the Vale of Rheidol, from Pendinas, to the National Library of Wales, Aberystwyth

the National Library of Wales away to your left. A legal deposit library containing millions of books, it was officially opened by King George VI and his Queen Elizabeth on 15 July 1937. Turn right to pass Plascrug School on your right and a rugby ground on your left, heading for the railway.

Cross the railway (**B**) with great care, going over the standard-gauge tracks of the line to Shrewsbury before the narrow-gauge track to Devil's Bridge. Go ahead through a small gate and along the narrow, metalled path that leads past a bridge over the River Rheidol on your right. Reach an isolated farmhouse on your left and continue along its access track to a road (Heol y Bont). Go right with it across the river (**C**).

Ignore the first road on your right (Min y Ddol) but turn right to take the second (Rhydbont). Look for a flight of steps between houses Nos. 56 and 58, on your left, and climb them to follow an enclosed path. Bear right at a fork, pass Bryn Ystwyth on your right, emerge on the A487 (First Avenue) and go left along its pavement to a post office. Turn right to cross the road by a zebra-crossing, go left for 20 yards (18 m) and turn right along a lane signposted as a public footpath, passing a pub called The Tollgate (**D**) on your left.

Turn right up a track immediately before a house called Gorwel Deg. The right-of-way continues as a hedged path. Cross a stile at its top, ignore a track on your right and take the right-hand of two narrow paths ahead, climbing with a fence on your right. The monument (**E**) on Pendinas is soon reached, giving a view over the River Ystwyth on your left.

Take the path towards modern Aberystwyth, keeping the sea on your left. Turn right when you meet a fence and descend along an enclosed path, ignoring gates into fields on either side. Turn left through a small metal gate and follow a hedged path down to the A487 (Penparcau Road). Go left downhill and then bear right along Trefechan Road to cross the bridge (**F**) over the River Rheidol, which affords a view of the harbour on your left.

Turn left along South Road to reach Aberystwyth's South Beach. Go right to pass the castle and war memorial on your right, walking along the New Promenade with the sea on your left. Pass the University College of Wales' original building on your right, then the pier on your left. Turn inland when you reach a zebra-crossing (**G**) and follow Terrace Road back towards the station. Visit the Ceredigion Museum and the tourist information centre, on your left immediately after Bath Street. The 'Aberystwyth Yesterday' exhibition, which is housed above the railway station, is also well worth a visit. □

10 Knighton

Start:	Knighton
Distance:	4½ miles (7.25 km)
Approximate time:	2 hours
Parking:	Knighton
Refreshments:	Tearooms and pubs at Knighton
Ordnance Survey maps:	Landranger 137 (Ludlow & Wenlock Edge) or 148 (Presteigne & Hay-on-Wye), Pathfinder 950, SO 27/37 (Knighton & Brampton Bryan) and 971, SO 26/36 (Presteigne)

General description *This walk climbs out of Knighton, where the railway station stands on the modern border between England and Wales. It follows the Offa's Dyke Path south, initially through woodland, then with fine views from a clear ridge, which is surmounted by the increasingly apparent earthworks of Offa's Dyke. The route returns to the town along another attractive woodland path. Try to allow time to visit the Offa's Dyke Heritage Centre Exhibition – near another good section of the dyke. Follow the signs, going along Broad Street, then bearing right along West Street.*

Knighton (**A**) is the 'town on the dyke' – Tref y Clawdd or Trefyclo in Welsh – and the modern frontier between Wales and England lies somewhere between the railway station platform and the car park. Step from the train in England, make for the exit to the road and you are in Wales. Things become clearer as you bear left to take the bridge over the River Teme to enter the town, along Station Road. Reach Broad Street and go left, then almost immediately right, along a road that passes a car park in the centre of the town.

Climb the road up to Ffrydd Terrace and follow the direction of an Offa's Dyke Path signpost, as if you were going to Nos. 31–42. Another sign on a lamppost directs you right, to pass garages on your left and the backs of gardens on your right. Bear left to cross a stile and head for the woodland (**B**).

Go ahead across a roughly metalled lane at the foot of the wood to continue climbing the path that is waymarked with the acorn symbol of the Offa's Dyke Path. The ancient earthwork is just about discernible on the right. Emerge from the woodland by going ahead over a stile and proceeding beside a fence on the right. The fence is on the line of Offa's Dyke, which is not as obvious here as 1 mile (1.5 km) further along this route. Some say that several different gangs of labourers built Offa's Dyke so the difference in height between this part and later in the walk may provide an example of one construction team being of a higher standard than another. Offa reigned over the Mercians from AD 757 to 796 and was probably inspired to have this mighty earthwork built after a Welsh attack in 784, whilst he was distracted by trying to become the ruler of the whole of England. The dyke probably testifies to an agreed border, although its ditch does face the Welsh side to give a defensive purpose

North-west from Offa's Dyke, south of Knighton

against the Welsh. A wooden palisade may have run along the top, and the whole route may have been patrolled. Evidence for the stable nature of this border is agreed laws on such things as cattle-rustling.

Go ahead over a series of waymarked stiles, keeping the fence on the right. The dyke becomes much more apparent, and a stile beckons you to cross it and the fence on your right to continue with the dyke on your left (**C**). Descend to the bottom of the third field after this switch to reach one of the original gateways through the dyke, near Jenkin Allis. Bear right with the waymarked path across two small fields, then along the right-hand side of two more fields to reach a road (**D**). Turn right down this to a junction with a lane on the right.

Turn right to follow this lane to Upper Woodhouse Farm, on the left (**E**). Bear right from the lane here, taking the sign-posted public footpath that crosses a stile beside a gate and leads to another stile by a gate. Continue along the top of a field sloping down to the left, with a hedge on the right. Go ahead over a stile in a fence ahead, having descended slightly from the line of the hedge.

Enter woodland, walking along the foot of the wooded slope. Descend to a lane, turn left over a cattle-grid in it and reach a road (**F**). Turn right along its pavement to return to the Offa's Dyke Path signpost near Ffrydd Terrace. Bear left down the small road you took on the way up. Pass the central car park, turn left into Broad Street, then turn right to follow Station Road back to the railway station and its car park.

Do not be surprised to see weary back-packers in Knighton. As well as the 177-mile (285 km) Offa's Dyke Path, the town is the southern terminus for Glyndŵr's Way. □

11 Caersws

Start:	Caersws
Distance:	5 miles (8 km)
Approximate time:	2½ hours
Parking:	Caersws
Refreshments:	Pubs and cafés at Caersws
Ordnance Survey maps:	Landranger 136 (Newtown & Llanidloes), Pathfinder 908, SO 09/19 (Newtown)

General description The village of Caersws is a strategic route centre. The Romans appreciated this and built a fort here – at the meeting-point of five roads. The village also stands on the bank of the River Severn, and the railway junction at Moat Lane was nearby. The train still reaches Caersws, which has a station on the surviving line between Shrewsbury and Aberystwyth. There are hills all around to provide fine backdrops, but these paths give level walking across fields and over stiles, with a fairly quiet road forming the final leg back into the village.

Starting from Caersws railway station, do not cross the track from the single platform. Take the road going away from the level-crossing and turn right to follow the road to the crossroads in the centre of the village. The car park is on your right, opposite the church. Go left along the pavement of the A470 and pass the grassy banks that mark where the walls of the Roman fort stood **(A)**.

Cropmarks spotted from the air in 1958 revealed an earlier Roman fort near the sewage works on the north-eastern side of Caersws. This probably functioned during the initial Roman thrust into mid Wales in the first century. The second fort, lying between the railway station and the A470 on the western side of the village, was probably built by AD 78. Its name links

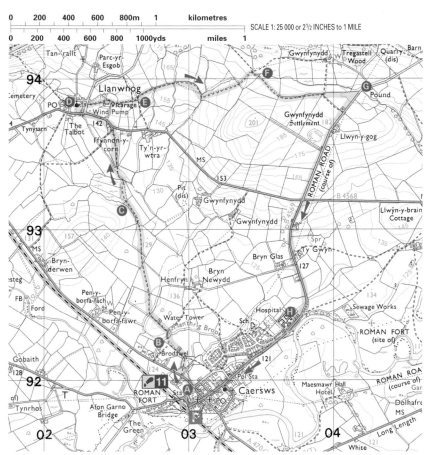

SCALE 1: 25 000 or 2½ INCHES to 1 MILE

The path going north from Caersws to Llanwnog

the prefix *caer* 'Roman camp' with the suffix *-sws*, derived from *Swswen*, a local queen. The railway now covers the southern corner of the fort, and a large Roman bath-house was found there in 1854 when the railway was built. The walls of the fort were rebuilt in red Kerry sandstone around AD 150, having originally been ramparts of stacked turfs with timber facing. Occupation continued until the fourth century.

Pass Manthrig Lane on your right, then an access lane to Hafod and bear right over a stile immediately after this to follow the signposted public footpath. Cross the field and a waymarked stile in the hedge ahead – which is on the site of the northern wall of the Roman fort. Continue beside a hedge on your left and bear left over a footbridge and a subsequent stile. Keep to the left-hand edge of the next field. Go ahead over another waymarked stile, about 50 yards (46 m) to the right of the corner on your left. A footbridge over Manthrig Brook leads to the corner of the next field (**B**).

Continue beside a hedge on your left, turn left over a waymarked stile and keep with a hedge on your left in the next field. Go ahead over a stile in the bottom left-hand corner. This is followed by a substantial, wooden footbridge. Bear right to take another stile, then a waymarked stile beside a gate in the far corner of the following field. The wooded hill of Alltwnnog, overlooking the village of Llanwnog and its church, is in front of you. Head towards it, through waymarked gates. A stile (**C**) gives access to a marshy field.

Skirt the bog to continue over a stile, take an isolated footbridge over a seasonal stream in the next field and find another footbridge in the shade of a willow-tree to go ahead over a stile and

walk with a hedge on your left. Bear left through a waymarked gap to follow the hedge on your right to a gate giving access to a road, which you turn left along to reach the village of Llanwnog. Pass a lane on your right but take the path on your right to St Gwynog's Church (**D**). The gifted Welsh poet Ceiriog Hughes is buried in the churchyard. He was once the stationmaster at Caersws. He was also the author of the hymn 'Jerusalem':

My cry is for my city
As desert sands I plod,
Jerusalem, my homeland,
The city of my God.

Facing the church porch, go right, to leave the churchyard by its other path. Go left at the lane and almost immediately turn right to follow a signposted public footpath. Pass to the left of a house, cross a waymarked stile and follow a hedge on your left. Bear left through a gate to put the hedge on your right. Continue over a stile in the next corner (**E**).

Walk beside the hedge on your left, cross a series of stiles and reach a stile on your left after the hedge has curved right. Turn left and go up a field to a waymarked gate. Reach a waymarked stile in the far neck of the next field (**F**).

Turn half right to cross the next field diagonally, bear left through a waymarked gate and follow a hedge on your left. At the end of the second field, go ahead over a waymarked stile and follow a hedge on your left to reach a gate giving access to a road (**G**).

Turn right to follow the road over a crossroads and back into Caersws. The hospital on your right (**H**) was once a large Poor Law institution. Divert left along the A470 if you wish to view the River Severn from the bridge before completing this walk. ☐

37

12 Llanerfyl

Start:	Llanerfyl
Distance:	5 miles (8 km)
Approximate time:	2½ hours
Parking:	Llanerfyl
Refreshments:	Shop and garage at Llanerfyl
Ordnance survey maps:	Landranger 125 (Bala & Lake Vyrnwy), Pathfinder 887, SJ 00/01 (Llanfair Caereinion)

General description *Most of this walk is along old cart-tracks or lanes, climbing to give views, then passing some attractive woodland. The delightful Afon Banwy is seen near the end of the walk. Allow time to acquire the key to the church, where an interesting tombstone is kept. Its inscription suggests that there was a woman priest here in the sixth century. Rosteece,* who seems to have died at the age of 63, was known as Erfyl. The patron saint of this parish, she was the daughter of St Padarn.

There is an official car park on your left as you enter Llanerfyl along the A458 from Welshpool. This is across the road from the garage. You can come here by bus, taking the S280 (Daffodil Line), which runs between Tywyn and Shrewsbury, or post-bus No. 108 from Welshpool. Roman roads from Neath to Chester, via Caersws, and Wroxeter to Brithdir (for Sarn Helen) crossed here, giving access for St Erfyl and her cousin St Cadfan (at nearby Llangadfan).

Go right from the car park and turn right down the road for Talerddig. Pass lanes on your right and left, pass the school on your left, ignore a road on your right and reach houses on both sides of your road at Diosg **(A)**. Just before a house named Llwynteg on your right, bear right up a hedged green lane. Bear right when this joins a metalled lane. Pass a track on your

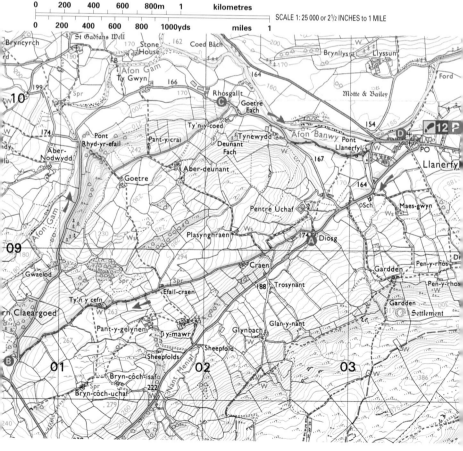

SCALE 1:25 000 or 2½ INCHES to 1 MILE

St Erfyl's Church, Llanerfyl

right giving access to Plasynghraen. Go straight ahead along the lane to Craen, where you pass the farm buildings on your left and continue along an enclosed path, with a view over the valley on your left. Maintain this direction when the surface becomes firm again and pass a house called Tŷ'n y Cefn on your right. Descend to a junction with a quiet lane (**B**).

Turn right down the lane, which soon acquires a strip of grass growing down its middle. Reach a junction with another lane coming across a bridge over the Afon Gam on your left. Turn right to go over a waymarked stile next to a gate opposite the bridge. Bear slightly right across pasture to a stile on the edge of woodland. Go ahead over it and up the wooded slope. Continue with a hedge on your left to a gate in the top left-hand corner of the field above the trees.

Turn left through this gate, ignore the access track to Goetre, on your right, and go ahead along a firm lane. Reach a road (**C**). Go right along it and soon pass the farm of Tynewydd on your right. Fork left down a signposted public bridleway, emerging above a river, the Afon Banwy, on your left. Continue across a ridge and on up the access lane of houses to a T-junction with another lane. Go left along this lane to the A458, joining it near the bridge over the Banwy, Pont Llanerfyl, on your left.

Turn right to walk with the A458 through Llanerfyl, passing the shop and post office on your left. Pass the church on your left to reach the garage, again on your left, at the far end of the village, where it is possible to obtain the key for the church. The car park is across the road from this garage.

St Erfyl's Church (**D**) is well worth a visit. Pride of place goes to its Romano-British tombstone, kept at the back. There are explanatory notes on the wall near the door. The monument is a roughly quadrangular pillar-stone, which originally stood in the churchyard. It has a Latin inscription in seven lines, reading horizontally: 'Here in the tomb lies Rosteece, daughter of Paterninus, aged 63 [easily misread as 13], in peace'. The letters are in Roman capitals similar to the style found in Italy in the fourth century and occurring in this country in the fifth and sixth centuries. The mention of the name of a dead person is rare. Local tradition has always connected the stone with the female patron saint of this parish, St Erfyl. Her real name appears to have been Rosteece, and her father, Paterninus, was St Padarn. The name Erfyl, meaning 'golden lip', seems to have been bestowed upon her as testimony to her eloquence. Could it be that the ancient Celtic Church had a woman priest in Llanerfyl? ☐

13 Tregaron

Start: Tregaron

Distance: 5 miles (8 km)

Approximate time: 2½ hours

Parking: Tregaron, near the statue and the Talbot Hotel

Refreshments: Pubs and cafés at Tregaron

Ordnance Survey maps: Landranger 146 (Lampeter & Llandovery), Pathfinders 968, SN 66/76 (Bronnant & Pontrhydfendigaid) and 990, SN 65/75 (Tregaron & Llanddewi-Brefi)

General description *This walk leaves from the place that put George Borrow 'very much in mind of an Andalusian village overhung by its sierra' and then climbs gradually with farm tracks to look across Cors Caron, the great bog. The odds are that you will see at least one red kite in the sky. A quiet lane leads back to Tregaron.*

Face the statue of Henry Richard in the centre of Tregaron (**A**). Erected in 1893, this commemorates the man who was born here in 1812 and became known as the 'Apostle of Peace' before his death in 1888. His career took him far from home, serving as minister of the Marlborough Congregational Church, London, from 1835 to 1850. The significant year of 1848 saw him appointed secretary of the Peace Society, and the boy from Tregaron play-ed a leading role in the peace conferences held in Brussels, Paris and Frankfurt over the next couple of years. A close friend of Richard Cobden and John Bright, he edited the *Herald of Peace*, the monthly magazine of the Peace Society. He also set out to interpret Welsh life to the English, becoming known as the 'Member for Wales' after his election to Parliament for the Merthyr Tydfil constituency in 1868. He protested against the 'Treachery of the Blue Books' in 1847 and maintained an interest in education, as well as religion. The Land Question also occupied him. Tenants evicted from their farms because of their religious and political beliefs were championed by him, as was the Ballot Act of 1872.

Turn around, putting the Talbot Hotel at your back and go ahead to pass the post office on the right. Cross the bridge over the River Brennig. Turn right with the B4343 road, signposted for Pontrhyd-fendigaid. Ignore a lane that is signposted as leading to a youth hostel on the right. Go ahead along the pavement of the B4343, ignoring a road serving the estate of Pwllswyddog on the right. Having left the town behind, bear right at a fork (**B**) towards Sunnyhill. At the time of writing, a beech tree marks this fork.

Pass Sunnyhill Farm on the right, con-tinue with the lane and turn left with it to walk with open pasture on the left and a fence on the right. The view on the left takes in the bog of Cors Caron. Ice move-ments during the last major glacial period created this broad basin of the River Teifi. A terminal moraine blocked the valley at Tregaron, causing a shallow lake to form above it. This slowly filed with sediments and vegetation. Reeds succeeded the open-water plants and their remains created the fen peat.

Tregaron, nestling in the valley of the Teifi

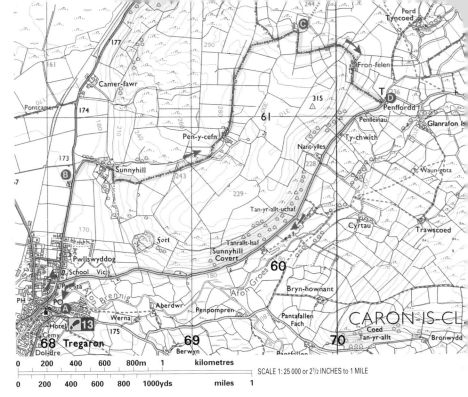

Continue past the farm of Pen-y-cefn. The lane becomes a firm track. Pass a little pond on the right and make sure not to be misled by a muddy path ahead when the firm track bears right. Descend to a track junction, where you go ahead, ignoring the track on the left.

Reach another farmhouse, on the left (**C**). Do not go through the gate and along the track ahead. Do turn right through another gate to take a grassy track between a fence on the left and a marshy space on the right. Do not go through the gate ahead at the next corner. Instead, turn left to walk with a hedge on the right in the next field. Continue with a hedge on the left and another field on the right. Pass a ruin surrounded by trees on the right.

Go ahead along a grass track with a fence on the left and at the foot of a bare slope on the right. Overlook some boggy land on the left. Take a gate in the corner ahead and carry straight on along the top of this small field, beside a fence on the right. Do not be tempted down the slope on the left. Bear right with the fence to another gate in the corner, with a small plantation of conifer trees on the left. Go past the farm of Fron-felen, passing the farmhouse on the right. Emerge in the corner of a field and turn left with a hedge on the left downhill. The Cambrian Hills are in front of you, contrasting with the bog seen earlier.

Reach a quiet lane (**D**) and turn right along it to walk back into Tregaron. When you reach the B4343, turn left to retrace your steps back to Henry Richard's statue and the Talbot Hotel, where George Borrow noted in his *Wild Wales* (1862) that he 'experienced very good entertainment ... had an excellent super and a very comfortable bed'.

Tregaron was a busy little place before the railway was built with the aid of bales of wool and wood faggots across Tregaron Bog to it in 1866 – being the line linking Aberystwyth with Carmarthen that was closed in 1965. Drovers used to assemble their stock here before crossing the mountains to England. They also helped the prosperity of the local cottagers by carrying samples of Tregaron socks and gloves. Financial services for the drovers were provided in the early nineteenth century by the Bank of the Black Sheep (Banc y Ddafad Ddu). The collapse of this bank in the depression following the Napoleonic Wars must have had a traumatic effect on the locals who were paid only 6s. 8d. (33.3p) for every £1 owed in 1827.

St Caron's Church rises from an oval mound that suggests a pre-Christian sacred site but is said to be the burial mound of St Caron. Among the interesting tombstones is that of Elizabeth Jones (d. 1726). It reads: 'Sooner or later go we must / Into our den beneath the dust'. □

14 Bucknell

Start:	Bucknell
Distance:	5 miles (8 km)
Approximate time:	2½ hours
Parking:	Near Bucknell Station
Refreshments:	Pub, restaurant and shop in Bucknell
Ordnance Survey maps:	Landrangers 137 (Ludlow & Wenlock Edge) or 148 (Presteigne & Hay-on-Wye), Pathfinder 950, SO 27/37 (Knighton & Brampton Bryan)

General description This walk takes firm tracks into the forest on Bucknell Hill, where there are still patches of native broadleaved trees. Bilberries ripen here in late summer and give sustenance for the descent past Honeyhole to the road above the River Redlake. A woodland path leads above the river back towards the village and provides ideal spots for picnics as well as – if you are lucky – views of kingfishers.

Starting from Bucknell Station, on the scenic Heart of Wales line, use the level-crossing to go over the railway from the side with the station platform. Walk left at a T-junction to follow a road that bends right to pass a school on your left and reach St Mary's Church (**A**) on your right.

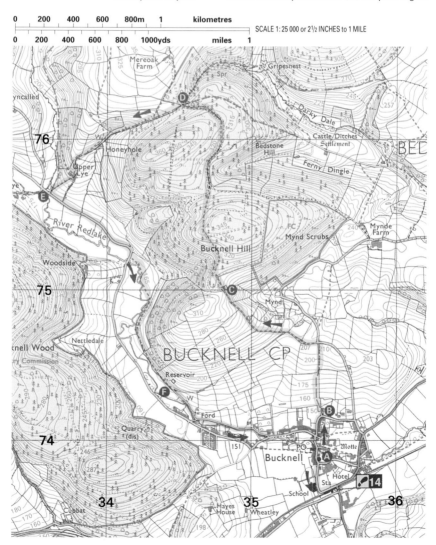

SCALE 1: 25 000 or 2½ INCHES to 1 MILE

The village of Bucknell from the slopes of Bucknell Hill

Continue across a bridge over the River Redlake, reach a junction of roads and go straight ahead along Dog Kennel Lane, passing a telephone-box on its corner to the right. Shortly after this lane bears right, turn left up a signposted bridleway, immediately before a house named Brookside (**B**). Continue through a gate and up an old, hollow way, then uphill along the right-hand side of a field. Take a gate in the corner to continue with the hollow way, then go along the left-hand edge of a field until a gate ahead gives access to a lane.

Turn left along the lane, which is soon signed as a 'no through road'. Pass Willow Cottage on the right, after which the lane deteriorates to a hedged track. Ignore tracks to left and right. Go ahead, climbing, to pass the gate of a house called Heavens Above on the right. Reach the entrance to the forest on Bucknell Hill (**C**).

Bear right at the sign warning about mountain bikes in the forest. Ignore a track soon afterwards on the right to keep straight on with the main track. Follow it over the brow of the hill and bear slightly right as it descends. Go ahead at a crosstracks and continue to reach a junction of forest tracks where a Forestry Commission sign says 'Hopton Caution! Mountain Bikes' (**D**). Another sign points ahead to Mereoak Farm.

Turn left through a wooden kissing-gate next to a field gate and walk along the left-hand edge of a field that has a shed on its right-hand side. Descend to cross a stile to the left of a gate ahead. Continue over a stile to the right of the next gate, as you descend. Bear left to pass the buildings of Honeyhole on your left and follow a track past the farm of Upper Lye on the right. Descend with this track to the road in the valley of the River Redlake (**E**).

Turn left along the road, above the river on the right. Immediately before a bridge across the river, turn left through a field gate to follow a signposted path through the meadow, with the river on the right. Cross a stile where a hedge ahead meets the river. Gradually bear left uphill to cross a stile and enter woodland on a bank above the river on the right. Turn right along a path that runs along the foot of the wooded slope on the left and overlooks the river on your right. Continue through a gate to reach a lane at a hairpin bend (**F**).

Fork right to take a metal gate across the lane and continue past a footbridge across the river on the right. Pass Seabridge Cottage on your right and follow Bridgend Lane to the road at Bucknell. Go left along the pavement to pass a restaurant on the left and return to the junction where Dog Kennel Lane is now on the left, with the telephone-box on its corner.

Turn right to walk past the church on your left as you retrace your steps to Bucknell's railway station. □

15 Moel Geufron

Start:	Roadside car park (map ref. SN 899720) near a bridge over a tributary of the River Elan ½ mile (0.75 km) west of the Aberystwyth–Rhayader mountain road's junction with the road through the Elan valley
Distance:	5½ miles (8.75 km)
Approximate time:	3 hours
Parking:	Near the bridge at the start
Refreshments:	None
Ordnance Survey maps:	Landranger 147 (Elan Valley & Builth Wells), Pathfinder 948, SN 87/97 (Llangurig & the River Wye)

General description *This walk strides over the moors and descends to the beautiful valley of the River Wye. A good track leads back up to the plateau, where it is a simple task to strike ahead and reach the old coach road that linked Aberystwyth and Rhayader, leading back to the car park at the start of this walk in the wild, isolated 'green desert'.*

Drovers crossed the 'green desert' by the exciting road which leads to the start of this walk. No doubt the route was in use in prehistoric times, as well as when the Cistercian monks were travelling in this area from their bases at Strata Florida and Abbeycwmhir. An earlier Dark Age – 'Golden Age' might be more correct for the Celtic west – monastic community probably existed near the start of this walk. The non-celibate community would have offered rest and refreshment to travellers. The old 6 inches to 1 mile Ordnance Survey map of this area shows the start of this route as Aber Henllan 'confluence of the old religious settlement'.

Cross the bridge to its western side and turn right to walk north, away from the road, along a track. Keep the stream on the right as you walk up the valley. Ford a tributary and maintain your direction even when the firm track ends by bearing left toward a ruin (**A**). Mining probably took place in this area, principally for lead. When the reservoirs were planned at the end of the nineteenth century, such activities ended so that the gathering ground for the Elan valley would be free of pollution.

Reach the top of a side valley overlooking the Wye valley. Go down the right-hand side of this side valley. The valley of the Wye is the one on the right, ahead, rather than the Dernol valley, ahead and going to your left. As the track bears right around the hillside, look across the Wye valley to see the windmills of an

The Wye valley, with Bryntitli windfarm on the hills beyond

energy farm. Descend to a junction and turn sharply left to go down through a gate and to the bottom left corner of a field. Turn right to keep descending with a fence on the left and reach Pen-yr-ochr (**B**).

Continue past Pen-yr-ochr's farmhouse on the right along a firm track that joins a lane. Maintain your direction down this lane. Turn right at a junction and cross a stream. Descend with the lane to the side of the River Wye, on your left. Bear right to diverge from it, climbing slightly to a fork (**C**).

Bear right at the fork to follow an uphill track. Pass the farmhouse of Tŷ-mawr on the left and continue to a track junction. Fork left, across a stream. Take a gate to ascend with a track up the left-hand side of this valley. Walk with a fence on the right, where you overlook the valley, while the hillside slopes upward on the left.

When the fence on the right makes a right turn down the valley, go straight ahead up the track. As you climb, another fence ascends the side of the valley to come up on your right. Keep climbing over a stile beside a gate and fork left here (**D**) to take a higher path to the plateau.

Go ahead across the moorland. Reach an old boundary bank, go straight across it and maintain your direction to ford a stream at Rhyd y Gors. This is the sort of country where it would be no surprise to meet the 'Powys beast'. No mythical creature, this 'big cat' has been seen by many people in this area. Dark in colour and as big as a puma, it leaves a strong scent and bounds along at 60 mph (95 kph).

Go ahead to the mountain road (**E**) and turn right along it to return to the start of this walk, passing the road for the Elan valley on the left. Craig Goch is the reservoir that can be seen on the left. □

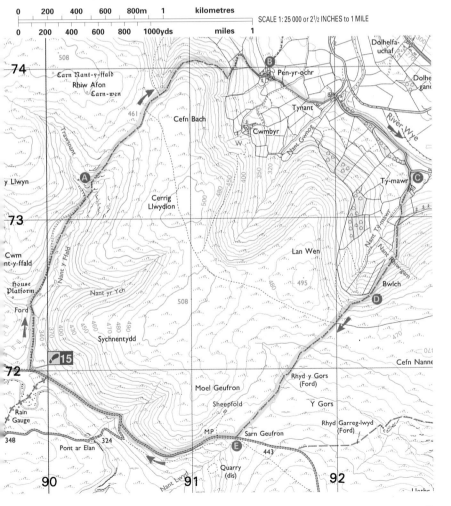

SCALE 1:25 000 or 2½ INCHES to 1 MILE

16 Llandrindod Wells

Start:	Llandrindod Wells
Distance:	6 miles (9.5 km)
Approximate time:	3 hours
Parking:	Llandrindod Wells
Refreshments:	Tearooms, pubs and cafés at Llandrindod Wells
Ordnance Survey maps:	Landranger 147 (Elan Valley & Builth Wells), Pathfinder 970, SO 06/16 (Llandrindod Wells)

General description *The spa town of Llandrindod Wells is a fine example of Victorian civilisation, complete with grand hotels and boating-lake. Come at the end of August to enjoy Victorian Week, re-creating the days when 80,000 visitors a year came here by the new railway. This walk climbs the hills to the east of the town for magnificent views in beautiful natural settings. It diverts across a bridge to visit the old church at Cefnllys before returning over hills and through wooded valleys to the capital of Powys.*

Starting from the railway station – on the side where trains leave for Llanelli and Swansea – go up Station Crescent to the centre of Llandrindod, passing the post office on your left. Go ahead at a cross-

roads to take Craig Road. This continues as Broadway. Reach Cefnllys Lane and turn left to pass Woodlands, an estate road, on the right, then pass Brookfields, another estate road, on the left. Turn right when you reach Hillside Lane (**A**), which is signposted as a public footpath.

Bear left, as signposted, along the fenced track when you reach the entrance to Hillside. Reach a signposted path junction and take a kissing-gate next to a field gate ahead, ignoring the signed path bearing through a kissing-gate on the left. After advancing 20 yards (18 m), go ahead up the left-hand of two signed paths and cross a stile to the left of a gate at the top of this field.

Go ahead along the well-trodden path, ignoring a signposted path going right. Keep climbing and cross four waymarked stiles to reach the 1,165-foot (355 m) summit of this hill. Continue down to a lane (**B**). Turn left along this to walk with a forest on the right. The lane bears right, descends and bears left away from the forest, soon deteriorating into a rough track. When this track turns right uphill, turn left over a stile and follow the signposted public footpath. This gradually converges with a fence on your left. Continue through a gate in the corner ahead and follow the clear path through bracken and woodland to emerge at a picnic place and car park beside a lane (**C**).

Turn left to a lane junction and turn right to cross the footbridge – still known as 'Shaky Bridge' although a sturdy struc-

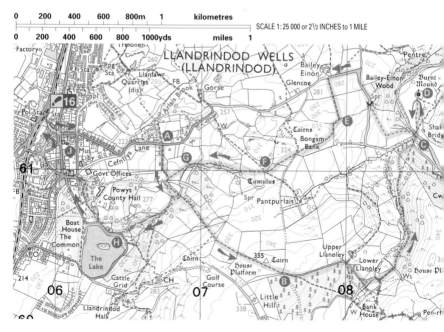

```
0   200   400   600   800m   1        kilometres
0   200   400   600   800   1000yds      miles   1
```
SCALE 1: 25 000 or 2½ INCHES to 1 MILE

The Ithon valley from the walk, above Shaky Bridge

ture has replaced the old suspension bridge – over the River Ithon. Follow the narrow, metalled path ahead to visit St Michael's Church (**D**). This firm access path was constructed in 1978 to mark the previous year's jubilee of Queen Elizabeth II's accession.

Retrace your steps to and across the footbridge. Go ahead through the gate, turn right immediately through another and bear left across a stile to follow the signposted path up pasture to a stile in the top fence giving access to a lane. Turn right along this lane and left with it, ignoring a 'no through road' ahead. When level with Bailey Einion on your right, turn left along a signposted path that keeps to the left-hand side of two fields. Cross a stile in the top fence, next to a gate and signpost (**E**).

Turn right, with the fence on your right. Continue over a stile in the corner and bear left, then swing across the field to walk with the hedge 50 yards (46 m) away on your left until it turns to meet your path at a corner marked by a signpost. Cut across a track to diverge from it and go over a stile into a plantation of conifer trees. Step over another stile to walk with the fence on the right until a waymarked stile (**F**) shows where you turn right

through this plantation to emerge at a stile on its far side.

Bear slightly left to descend and take a small metal gate in the fence on the left to follow a path through a wooded valley, with a stream on the left. A stile gives access to a road at a new housing estate (**G**). Go left to where the path bears left to the junction met on the outward route. Go left to the signpost at the foot of the sloping field, but this time fork right to a stile in the top right-hand corner.

Turn right to follow the signposted path past woodland on the left and with a fence on the right. Bear right at the next signpost and emerge from the wood at a lakeside road (**H**). Go right, with the lake on the left. Bear right through an ornate metal kissing-gate and follow the path that is signposted through woodland to pass Powys County Hall on the right.

Emerging at the road, go left, ignore a road on the right but turn right at a crossroads to follow Temple Street past the Hotel Metropole (**J**) on the right. The scant remains of the stone circle that earned this street its name are obscured by hedgerows breaking up the lawn on the left. Continue to the left down Station Crescent to return to Llandrindod Wells railway station. ☐

17 Sutton Walls

Start:	Moreton on Lugg
Distance:	6 miles (9.5 km)
Approximate time:	3 hours
Parking:	Moreton on Lugg, near St Andrew's Church or in St Peter's Close
Refreshments:	Pub at Marden, shops at Marden and Moreton on Lugg
Ordnance Survey maps:	Landranger 149 (Hereford & Leominster), Pathfinder 1017, SO 44/54 (Hereford North)

General description *Walking around this part of Herefordshire's central plain is easy, with just one gentle climb to the hill-fort known as Sutton Walls. There is a great sense of history, with the meadows having been grazed for thousands of years and the River Lugg bordered by old pollarded willows. Near the river stands Marden church, marking where King Offa buried Ethelbert, after having his prospective son-in-law and rival murdered.*

Begin at Moreton on Lugg, where there is a good bus service, especially from Hereford, to the turning from the A49. There should be a space to park a car in the village, where the route follows the main road past St Andrew's Church (**A**) on the right, then St Peter's Close on the left. Continue over a railway level-crossing and a bridge over the River Lugg.

About 50 yards (46 m) after Moreton Bridge, bear left over a stile to take the signposted public footpath through a meadow, with the River Lugg on your left. Aim to the right of the spire of Marden church, cross a stile (**B**) and bear slightly right in the next field. Continue over a stile to the left of a gate and maintain this direction to a flat, wooden bridge over a ditch. Go through the subsequent gate and keep near the right-hand side of this field to reach a stile beside a signpost about 50 yards (46 m) from the corner on your right. Ignoring the main road on the right, turn left along a 'no through road' signposted for Marden church. This church is at the end of the road (**C**).

Marden church was built on the orders of the Pope to mark the spot where the body of King Ethelbert of East Anglia was buried in 793. He had been murdered by King Offa, who ruled Mercia from a palace in the area, perhaps on the western side of Sutton Walls. Offa had tempted Ethelbert here with the prospect of his daughter's hand in marriage. Such a union would have increased Ethelbert's power to the detriment of Offa's, so Offa had Ethelbert murdered. Offa's conscience was then struck by the sight of a brilliant, supernatural light. He was moved to atone by giving one-tenth of his property to the Church and going on a pilgrimage to Rome. Ethelbert's body was later moved to the cathedral in Hereford.

Going right from the church porch, turn right around the back of the church, as directed by a signpost. Go ahead over a stile bearing the sign 'Central Avenue' and come to another stile, which you cross to emerge in the corner of a narrow field. Go ahead with an orchard on the right and the River Lugg on the left. The

Marden church from Sutton Walls

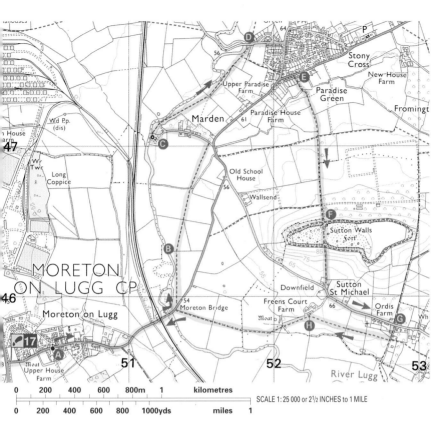

```
0    200   400   600   800m   1    kilometres
0    200   400   600   800   1000yds   miles   1
```

SCALE 1: 25 000 or 2½ INCHES to 1 MILE

river hereabouts is said to conceal a lost bell from the church, carried to the bottom by a mermaid.

Go ahead with the river on the left and maintain this direction when it makes a loop away to your left. When the hedge on the right ends at this point, go ahead over stiles in the wooden fences of a paddock to come close to the river on the left again before finally emerging on a road near Laystone Bridge, Marden (**D**).

Turn right along the road, passing Laystone Green on the left. Go right at a T-junction to follow the road signposted for Moreton on Lugg and Sutton St Nicholas. Pass Orchard Green on the right, then Walkers Green on the left. Reach a junction with a main road and go left for about 100 yards (91 m). Reach a signposted public footpath on the right, where there is a stile beside a gate (**E**). This enclosed path leads to the corner of a small field. Go along a fence on the right.

Take a gate ahead to enter the corner of the next field, where you continue with a fence on the left. Look for a stile in this fence and cross it, then turn right to maintain your direction with the fence on your right. Go ahead over a stile in a corner and soon cross wooden bars that serve as a

stile in the hedge on the right, then turn left to continue with the hedge on your left all the way to the wooded ring of Sutton Walls. Enter the old hill-fort over a stile (**F**). Decapitated skeletons found here probably date from when the Romans took the fort, whose single great ditch enclosed a thriving village.

Go straight ahead across the hill-fort and down the firm track towards Sutton St Michael. Turn left along the road here and soon ignore a lane on the right. Go past St Michael's Church, Sutton, on the right. Reach a crossroads where the lane on the left is signposted as a public bridleway and the lane on the right as a public footpath (**G**). Turn right down the lane until it loses its metalled surface and continues ahead as a hedged track.

Turn right at the end of the metalled lane to cross a stile and follow the signposted public footpath through three fields to a stile near Freens Court Farm (**H**). Cross this and bear left, walking with a hedge on the right to cross a footbridge over a ditch. Bear right and continue through meadows to return to the road near Moreton Bridge. Turn left to retrace your steps across the bridge and into Moreton on Lugg. □

18 Wynford Vaughan Thomas' Viewpoint

Start:	Aberhosan
Distance:	6 miles (9.5 km)
Approximate time:	3 hours
Parking:	Aberhosan, near postbus stop
Refreshments:	None
Ordnance Survey maps:	Landranger 135 (Aberystwyth) or 136 (Newtown & Llanidloes), Pathfinder 907, SN 89/99 (Penffordd-Las)

General description Aberhosan is an isolated hamlet in the shadow of Foel Fadian – at 1,850 feet (564 m) the highest peak in the old county of Montgomeryshire. It is the terminus for a post-bus from Machynlleth. A firm track makes a gradual ascent from here up to the memorial to Wynford Vaughan Thomas (1908–87). Finally, the route joins Glyndŵr's Way to descend to Aberhosan. Dedicate this outstanding walk to Wynford's memory and enjoy it with his characteristic 'pointless optimism'.

Begin by taking the road uphill out of Aberhosan, leaving the small housing estate and the terminus for the post-bus from Machynlleth on the right. Ignore a lane forking left, climb with the 'no through road' and reach Tŷ-gwyn on your right (**A**). The road deteriorates to a firm,

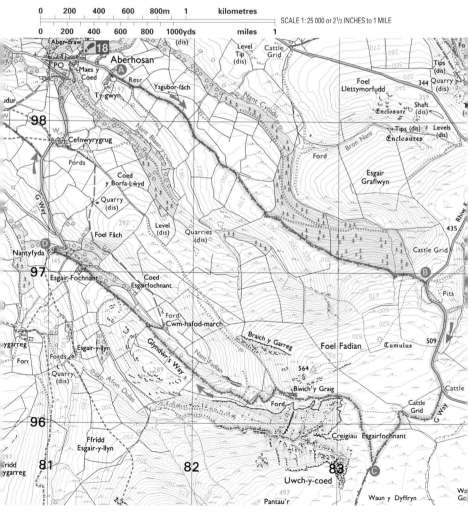

Glyndŵr's Way above Aberhosan

hedged track. Continue with this, climbing gradually. Go ahead through a gate to walk with open pasture on the right. Continue through another gate to walk with a fence on your right and open pasture on your left. Take the next gate across the track to walk with the perimeter fence of a forest on the left and open hillside rising on the right. After three more gates you arrive at the Wynford Vaughan Thomas memorial (**B**). This takes the form of a view indicator beside the mountain road running between Machynlleth and Staylittle. The Queen has been driven along this way to admire the tremendous views across the Dyfi valley to southern Snowdonia. The viewpoint was a favourite spot of the great writer, broadcaster and traveller.

An incongruously well-dressed crowd gathered at the unveiling of the memorial in May 1990. Its sculptured panel shows Wynford Vaughan Thomas in walking-gear pointing to Snowdon, which may

be visible on a clear day. Among the speakers at the ceremony was the opera singer Sir Geraint Evans.

Go right along the road, uphill, for ½ mile (0.75 km). Turn right with the sign-posted bridleway that forms part of Glyndŵr's Way. Go over a cattle-grid to follow a firm track towards the nature reserve and lake of Glaslyn. As Glaslyn approaches, you come to a signposted track junction (**C**). Turn sharply right here to follow the signposted bridleway that forms part of Glyndŵr's Way. Head towards Foel Fadian.

Pass a rocky gorge on the left and bear left, as waymarked, to descend to a gate. Continue along a downhill track with a valley on your right. This turns into a road at Nantyfyda (**D**). Bear right at a fork to follow the road back to Aberhosan. Turn right along a hedged path to cross a footbridge into the hamlet and then turn right up the road back to the start of this walk. □

19 Borth and Sarn Gynfelyn

Start:	Borth
Distance:	6 miles (9.5 km)
Approximate Time:	3 hours
Parking:	Borth
Refreshments:	Pubs and cafés at Borth
Ordnance Survey maps:	Landranger 135 (Aberystwyth), Pathfinder 926, SN 57/58 (Aberystwyth)

General description *The walk follows the spectacular cliff-top path from the seaside resort of Borth to the intriguing shingle ridge of Sarn Gynfelyn, said to be an ancient causeway belonging to the submerged land of Cantre'r Gwaelod. The route then takes a grassy lane inland to join the fairly quiet B4572 road back to Borth.*

Borth was changed from a tiny fishing hamlet to a resort – boasting a 4-mile (6.5 km) beach with a fossil forest at its northern end – with the coming of the railway in 1863. You can still arrive here by train on the line between Aberystwyth and Shrewsbury. Borth also has a good bus service to and from Aberystwyth, and the 108-mile (174 km) long-distance Dyfi

Valley Way terminates here.

Begin from the car park and bus-stop beside the life-boat station. Facing this, go left to walk with the sea on your right. Turn right along a 'no through road' to keep above the sea and at the end of the road continue along the cliff-top path. Reach the war memorial **(A)**.

Continue along the coastal path going south from Borth, keeping the sea on your right. Look out for Sarn Gynfelyn extending into the sea. Imagine, whilst walking above the sea, that you are overlooking a fertile plain. This would be the legendary Cantre'r Gwaelod 'Lowland Hundred'. Scientists agree that it did exist, perhaps around 3500 BC, when there may have been some earthquake or other natural disaster at a similar time to the submerging of land around the Scilly Isles that gave rise to the legend of Lyonesse. If so, the rich legends of its drowning are extremely old. These are usually reckoned to date from about AD 500.

Sarn Gynfelyn extended from Wallog to the principal settlement of Cantre'r Gwaelod, Caer Wyddno, the city of Gwyddno Garanhir, who protected his territory with sea walls and appointed Seithenyn as a gate-master. One night Seithenyn was drunk and neglected his duties, with the result that the sea broke through and drowned the land. The drunkard's sons tried to atone for their negligent father by taking holy orders, so they can be traced to sixth-century churches. Gwyddno ended his days as an

Wallog from the end of Sarn Gynfelyn at low tide

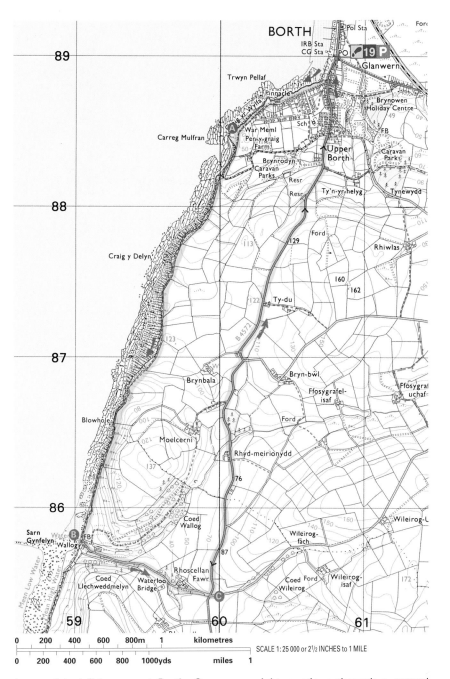

impoverished fisherman at Borth. One day his son, Elphin, fished a baby boy out of the River Dyfi and named him Taliesin – but that is another story.

Descend to the start of Sarn Gynfelyn at Wallog (**B**). Cross a footbridge over the stream here and leave the coastal path by turning left inland along a track. Go through a gate, pass below a house on your right, continue through a second gate and keep with this track all the way to its junction with the B4572 road (**C**). Turn left to follow this road the 2½ miles (4 km) back to Borth. If conditions permit, you could extend this walk by continuing along the beach past the fossil forest to Ynyslas Nature Reserve, which is situated at the mouth of the River Dyfi. □

20 Devil's Bridge

Start:	Devil's Bridge Railway Station
Distance:	6½ miles (10.5 km)
Approximate time:	3½ hours
Parking:	Devil's Bridge
Refreshments:	Hotel, café and shop at Devil's Bridge
Ordnance Survey maps:	Landranger 135 (Aberystwyth), Pathfinder 947 SN 67/77 (Devil's Bridge & Llanilar)

General description *This walk through the beautiful, tranquil valley of the River Mynach starts from the railway station, and there is no better way to arrive here than by steam train from Aberystwyth. Fieldpaths lead to woodland tracks, cross two footbridges and return down the valley past old lead mines. Allow time to visit the famous Devil's Bridge at the end.*

Cross the road from the entrance to the Devil's Bridge terminus of the Vale of Rheidol Railway. Pass the Welsh Craft Shop on your right as you take a track

ahead. Soon fork left, go ahead through a gate and along a fenced path. Continue over a stile to reach a corner of a forestry plantation ahead. Bear left across a field and pass a house on your left as you bear right across a waymarked stile. Continue to another stile that gives access to a road near a public footpath signpost (**A**). Go right along this road.

Bear left through a gate to take the signposted bridleway for Aber Bodcoll. Almost immediately, fork left down a public footpath, waymarked by a yellow arrow. This leads through woodland to a footbridge across the River Mynach. Go left over this to pass what remains of Bodcoll Mill and climb to pass crags on your right, then cross a stile to the right of a gate ahead. Continue with a fence on your left.

Approach woodland and reach a waymark post (**B**). Turn right uphill, as waymarked. Turn right at a higher waymark post and cut across a track to maintain height and enter a patch of woodland at another waymark post. Bear left at the top of crags to walk above a valley on your right. Follow the path to a stile beside a gate giving admission to a forest. Go over this and along a forest path that gradually descends to converge with a track coming from your right. Continue up the valley,

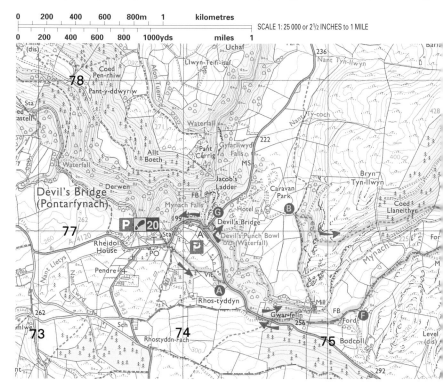

SCALE 1:25 000 or 2½ INCHES to 1 MILE

with the river on your right.

Follow the waymarked forest track to pass above Llaneithyr (**C**) on your right. Take a stile beside a gate ahead and fork right along the lower track to put trees on your left and a view over the Mynach on your right. Pass a confluence on your right and rise with the track. Look for a waymark post on your right (**D**) and turn right, downhill, as directed by its yellow arrow.

Cross a footbridge over a stream and a subsequent stile. Bear right, as way-marked, to reach isolated trees marking a gap in an old field boundary. Turn right downhill to a footbridge (**E**), to the left of the confluence. Continue over it and take a ladder-stile on your right to walk with the stream on your right, keeping the perimeter fence of the forest on your left.

Continue downstream to cross a stile beside a gate and walk inside the forest fence. Emerge from the forest to keep beside the river on your right. Follow a track that diverges from a fence and the river on your right. Pass remains of old lead mines on your left. A track sign-posted as a private road comes sharply from your left to converge with yours. Continue with the valley on your right and ignore another private road coming in sharply from your right.

Follow the path through Coed Llaneithyr

When the track forks (**F**), take the lower track, which is waymarked with a blue arrow. Continue across a footbridge over a tributary stream. Pass Aber Bodcoll and return to the road. Go right, towards Devil's Bridge.

Pass the signposted footpath of your outward journey on your left, then a car park for people visiting Devil's Bridge. At the road junction, where the Hafod Arms Hotel is on your left, divert right to visit Devil's Bridge (**G**). You will have to pay to see the Mynach Falls, immortalised by Wordsworth, as well as Jacob's Ladder, the Robber's Cave and, of course, the bridge, which was, according to tradition, built by the devil. When he tried to claim the soul of the first woman to cross it, she spotted his cloven hoof and sent her dog instead.

Turn back to the road junction and go right, passing the Hafod Arms Hotel on your left, to reach the railway station. The Vale of Rheidol Railway is now owned by the Brecon Mountain Railway Company, which runs a seasonal steam-hauled service from Aberystwyth (Tel: 01970 625819). The gauge is 1 foot 11½ inches (60 cm), and the line climbs over 600 feet (183 m) on its journey of 11¾ miles (19 km) from Aberystwyth. Built to extract lead and timber from this attractive valley, this line has carried passengers since 1903, only a year after its opening for goods traffic. □

21 Moreton and Stockton

Start:	Layby on the left (½ mile (0.75 km) north of the junction of the A49 with the A4112
Distance:	7 miles (11.25 km)
approximate time:	3½ hours
Parking:	Layby (above)
Refreshments:	Pub in Stockton
Ordnance Survey: maps:	Landranger 149 (Hereford & Leominster) Pathfinder 972, SO 46/56 (Tenbury Wells & Mortimer's Cross)

General description *Much of this walk is along paths or old green lanes that have a belt of woodland on one side and open fields and views on the other. Berrington Hall is not seen, but its estate is encircled. Traditional 'black and white' houses and fields of soft fruit give the flavour of Herefordshire.*

Go left from the layby along the verge of the A49 and pass Park Farm on your left. When level with a tree about 100 yards (91 m) after the farm, bear left down the slope to a waymarked gate beside a signpost (**A**). Go through this into the field and cross it diagonally to take a gate in the far right-hand corner. Maintain this direction in the next field, where a fence soon appears on your right. Go ahead through a gate and cross open meadow, passing a copse on the right.

The boundary fence of the Berrington Estate can be seen in the hedge on the right. Continue through a gate and over a footbridge to follow an old green lane. As the views become more open, notice the line of the old Mamble Canal away to your left. Eventually, a hedged track leads into Moreton, passing a typical 'black and white' farmhouse – a traditional timber-framed building (**B**).

Go straight across the road to take a track signposted as a public bridleway. Pass a forestry plantation on the left. When the bridleway turns left, bear with a fieldpath and keep the hedge on your left all the way to a lane (**C**).

Turn right along the lane, passing a recently created fish-pond on the far side of the hedge on the left. A castle used to occupy the site above it. Notice Ashton Fruit Farm on your right. As well as 'pick your own' fruit, there is a seasonal fruit-stall during the summer months. Turn right along the A49 through Ashton, passing the access road for Berrington Hall on the right. Turn left when you come to Hundred Lane, signposted for The Hundred and Middleton on the Hill (**D**).

Soon turn right off Hundred Lane, taking a bridleway whose signpost is across the road. Emerge in the corner of a field and walk with a hedge on the right. Maintain this direction through a series of gates and with a hedge on your right until the path is enclosed by a fence on the left as well. Go ahead to reach the A4112 at Stockton (**E**), where there is a pub.

Turn right along the road to its junction with the A49 and go right along the verge of this road to the layby where this route starts. □

Moreton Farm

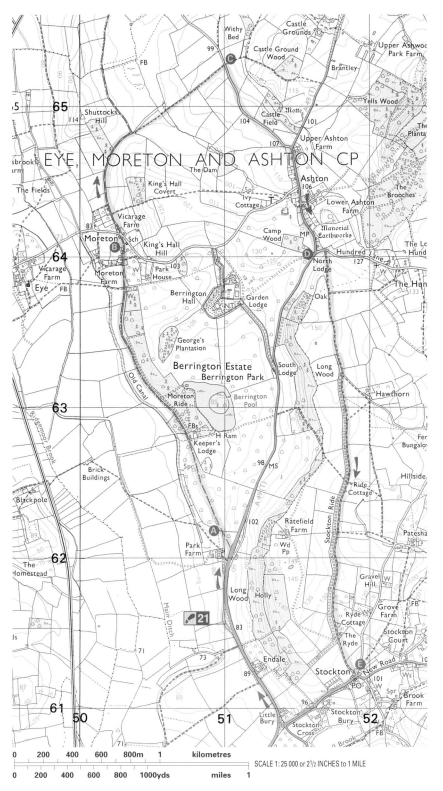

22 Cilmery

Start:	Cilmery (Cilmeri)
Distance:	8½ miles (13.5 km)
Approximate time:	4 hours
Parking:	Layby at the monument, Cilmery
Refreshments:	Pub at Cilmery
Ordnance Survey maps:	Landranger 147 (Elan Valley & Builth Wells), Pathfinder 992, SO 05/15 (Builth Wells)

General description To see the silvan banks of the Wye at their most colourful, take this walk in autumn. The route follows part of the waymarked Wye Valley Walk from the spectacular Pen-ddôl Rocks upstream past meadows and woodland until a path turns across a field to link with the lane back to the pleasant farm access track for Cilmery. It also passes the monument to the last Welsh Prince of Wales.

Cilmery has a station on the Heart of Wales railway line. If you start here, follow the access track up to the A483 road. Turn left along this road, passing the Prince Llewelyn Inn on your left. Bear left, with

SCALE 1:25 000 or 2½ INCHES to 1 MILE

The River Wye near Cilmery

the A483, at a fork and look for the large standing stone monument on your left. Cars may be parked in the layby here (**A**).

Prince Llywelyn ap Gruffydd was the first as well as the last Welsh Prince of Wales – not counting Owain Glyndŵr. He was formally recognised by King Henry III of England in 1267. The accession of Edward I led to Llywelyn having to pay homage to the King in London in 1277. The experience was so humiliating that Llywelyn resolved to fight rather than suffer such derision again. The rising came in 1282. One notable Welsh lord who held back from supporting Prince Llywelyn was Gruffydd ap Gwenwynwyn of southern Powys.

Hostilities began in March, and Edward soon mobilised a mighty force to deal with the rising, making Chester his base. Llywelyn did little until after the birth of his daughter, Gwenllian, in June. His beloved wife, Eleanor, the daughter of Simon de Montfort, died giving birth to her sixty-year-old husband's only child. The Prince now hoped that the blood of his enemies would wash away his sorrows. Peace proposals were rejected in November, and Llywelyn determined to bring south Powys back under his rule.

On the morning of 11 December 1282, the Welsh army moved to take Builth and came face to face with an English army at Irfon Bridge. There seemed that there would be no fighting that day, so the Prince chose to slip away, perhaps to clinch a deal for some promised new support. In his absence, the English took the bridge and, as dusk fell, scattered encounters took place. The returning prince was mortally wounded in one of these by a contingent of English horsemen led by Stephen Frankton.

Face the monument and go left to take the A483 back into Cilmery. Continue past the access track to the station on your right. Just before the road rises to cross the railway, turn left along a lane, which passes the small estate of Cefn Llewelyn (**B**) on the left and goes downhill to cross a stream by a bridge; the right-of-way uses a ford. Rise up through the yard to Neuadd-rhos-Fer Farm. Bear right and go through the right-hand of two gates to descend with an enclosed track to the railway embankment (**C**). Continue to a road at Rhoscwm (**D**).

Turn right along the road and turn left at a signpost for a public bridleway (**E**). Follow this path to the River Wye, where you turn left along the Wye Valley Walk, keeping the river on your right. Continue under the railway bridge. The waymarked route bears right to cross a footbridge over a tributary stream (**F**) when level with Dolyrerw Farm, which is across the fields on your left.

Continue with the river on the right and reach a track that leads ahead at the foot of a wooded slope on the left. Pass below a house on the left and go ahead, as waymarked, over a stile in the wooden fence before a meadow. Walk along the long, narrow meadows, keeping the river on your right. Reach a signpost preceding a footbridge and a stile (**G**). Cross the footbridge and stile and bear left, uphill and away from the River Wye. Climb the wooded slope to a corner of pasture. Go ahead across this pasture to a stile in the hedge opposite. This gives you access to a road.

Turn left along the road and continue for 1.5 miles (2.5 km) to Rhoscwm, where you turn right to retrace your steps down the farm access track back to Cilmery. □

23 Abbeycwmhir

Start:	Abbeycwmhir
Distance:	6½ miles (10.5 km)
Approximate time:	3 hours
Parking:	Abbeycwmhir, opposite St Mary's Church
Refreshments:	Pub and shop at Abbeycwmhir
Ordnance Survey maps:	Landranger 136 (Newtown & Llanidloes) or 147 (Elan Valley & Builth Wells), Pathfinder 949, SO 07/17 (Llanbister & Abbeycwmhir)

General description *This remote, long valley attracted the Cistercians to build an abbey. Now in ruins, it claims the headless body of Llywelyn the Last. The walk strikes north along forest tracks and paths to emerge on a quiet lane. It follows this back in the company of Glyndŵr's Way and cuts across fields above an interesting old house to return down forest tracks to the abbey ruins.*

Abbeycwmhir

Begin this walk from the Happy Union Inn at Abbeycwmhir, opposite St Mary's Church. The Happy Union Inn has a cheerful pub sign showing a man with a leek in his hat riding a goat and holding aloft a jug of ale. The church dates from 1680, when stone was taken for it from the nearby abbey ruins. It was entirely rebuilt, again with stone from the old abbey, in 1866. It is easy to pass by the ruins of the abbey, so be alert as you face the church and go right, soon passing a telephone-box on the right. Bear left with the road but halt at the first field gate on the right. This gives access to the abbey ruins, so divert through it and down a field to see them. The tranquil site and surrounding scenery are now more impressive than the ruins of Abbeycwmhir (**A**). Never completed, it was a victim of the wars between Welsh and English. It was intended to become the largest abbey in Wales. Only three ecclesiastical buildings in Britain – the cathedrals at Winchester, Durham and York – have naves exceeding the 242-foot (74 m) length of Abbeycwmhir's. The nave and aisles were completed, but the transept and chancel were never finished. The choir sang in part of the nave.

This was a Cistercian abbey, and the white-robed monks ate fish rather than flesh, so the proximity of the Clywedog Brook was crucial. A fish-pond remains, and there is evidence that the water was also used to power mills and flush away sewage. The abbey might have been capable of supporting up to sixty monks.

The original foundation may have been about 1 mile (1.5 km) to the east, dating from 1143, when the local lord was Maredudd ap Madog. The English conquered his lands in 1144, disrupting this first foundation. The abbey was re-founded on the present site in 1176, when the area was back in the Welsh hands of Cadwallon ap Madog, the cousin of Rhys ap Gruffydd, the prince of South Wales. The first monks came from the Cistercian Whitland Abbey in Dyfed, founded by Rhys ap Gruffydd. At the end of the twelfth century, Abbeycwmhir was to send monks to found Cymer Abbey, near Dolgellau, in Gwynedd.

By the start of the thirteenth century, the Mortimers had replaced the Welsh as patrons of the abbey. Their king, John, put the abbey under his protection in 1214 and granted the monks freedom from tolls on their own goods, so long as they bought nothing from and sold nothing to the king's enemies. Henry III was to remember the clause in 1231, when a friar was said to have helped the Welsh, under Llywelyn ab Iorwerth, to defeat the

English. The abbey had to pay a fine of 300 marks, on pain of being destroyed.

Tradition makes Abbeycwmhir a Welsh national shrine, for it is here that the headless body of Llywelyn the Last is said to be buried. No gravestone has ever been found to confirm this, but the last true-born Prince of Wales was killed in a skirmish near Builth on 11 December 1282. His severed head was sent with a report to Edward I. The Welsh poet Gruffydd ab yr Ynad Coch wrote in anguish:

See you not the rush of the wind and rain?
See you not the oaks thrashing each other?
See you not that the truth is portending?

See you not that the sun is hurtling the sky?
See you not that the stars have fallen?
Do you not believe in God, foolish men?
See you not that the world is ending?
Ah, God, that the sea would cover the land!
What is left us that we should linger? ...
Head cut off, no hate so dreadful,
Head cut off, thing better not done,
Head of a soldier, head of praise,
Head of a warlord, dragon's head,
Head of fair Llywelyn, harsh fear strikes the world,
An iron spike through it.

The abbey was sacked and destroyed by the Welsh patriot Owain Glyndŵr in

SCALE 1:25 000 or 2½ INCHES to 1 MILE

61

1401, probably because it was under the patronage of the Mortimers. A scorched earth policy was implemented against their estates. Edward IV was a descendant of the Mortimers and when he acceded in 1461, the abbey became crown property. It never acquired the wealth, or decadence, of other abbeys. At the Dissolution in 1536, its lands were valued at £24 19s. 4d. There were only three monks, which suggests that austerity was maintained.

The nave had a double row of fourteen arched bays, four more than at Wells Cathedral, which are said to have been as splendid as those at Canterbury. Luckily, five of the nave bays were incorporated in Llanidloes church when it was reconstructed in 1542.

The abbey came into the hands of William Fowler in 1565. Richard Fowler fortified it for the Royalists during the Civil War, but it was reduced by the Roundheads under Sir Thomas Middleton in 1644. The Fowlers were to retain their wealth and importance, as the old rhyme recorded:

Alas, Alas! poor Radnorshire,
Never a park, nor even a deer,
Nor ever a squire of five hundred a year,
Save Richard Fowler of Abbeycwmhir.

As well as using the abbey ruins as a quarry for building St Mary's Church, Richard Fowler took the stone to build his manor-house of Tŷ Faenor (Dyfaenor).

Return through the field gate to the road and go right to resume your previous direction. Soon fork left along a forest road that climbs to a junction. Turn sharply left along a rough forest track and pass above the hall that was built with stone taken from the abbey ruins by Thomas Wilson in 1833. Continue with an afforested slope rising on the right and rough pasture in an open space on the left. Pass a house on the right and go ahead with the track through the forest, climbing quite steeply to a junction of five tracks (**B**).

Forests are not the best places to get lost in and, while the right-of-way is clear, it was not waymarked when surveyed, so pay special attention to the directions from this point. Ignore the first track on your left and bear left along the second track. This soon comes to another junction where the main track goes right. Leave it by going left along the secondary track. After 100 yards (91 m), fork right along a narrower path through the forest. Descend to a firm forest track (**C**).

Go straight across the track to descend with the narrower, softer path. Reach another firm, broad track and turn right along it. Come to a fork where the main track starts to climb and bear right. Bear left here along the lower track. Look out for a gate in the perimeter fence on your left (**D**). Bear left from the track to go through it and go ahead with a stream, shaded by trees, on the left. Continue through a gate and beside a fence on the right and ignore another bridleway coming from across the field on the left. Go ahead to a lane.

Turn right along the lane and turn right again at a junction (**E**). Pass the farmhouse of Tŷ'n-y-berth on the left and follow this lane for over 2 miles (3.25 km). Although this is a metalled lane, there are few cars on it so it is an enjoyable walk, through a splendid valley. Gentle parkland stretches away to the left. Glyndŵr's Way follows this lane on its 120-mile (193 km) route from Knighton to Welshpool via Machynlleth.

Just as the lane bears slightly left downhill to the old manor-house of Tŷ Faenor (Dyfaenor), bear right to climb the bank to a stile in the fence (**F**). Go ahead over it and across a field above the manor-house on your left to a stile on the fence ahead. Continue along a clear path that gradually descends to a firm track coming up from your left. Take care here not to go ahead along this track that soon turns right and goes up the valley on the left. Do cross the track to bear left down a slope to a stile in the fence at its foot, which you cross to join Glyndŵr's Way at a waymark post (**G**).

Go right to follow the waymarked path through woodland. Cross a footbridge over a stream on the left and bear left with the path on the other side. Pass a gate with a 'private' sign on your right, bear left across an old, hollow way and climb to a waymarked stile. Cross it to walk with a fence on the right and soon turn right with the fence. Pass two field gates on your right. Bear right through the next waymarked gate and then climb to pass a house on the left. Descend to take a gate (**H**) giving access to a track that leads into the forest.

Follow the track into the forest and take care again not be seduced onto the wrong track. A road comes from the right to join yours. Bear left with it to maintain your direction. Continue down this road, ignoring the track forking right, which you should remember as the route of your outward journey. Descend to the road near the ruins of the old Cistercian abbey (**A**) and go right to retrace your steps back to the Happy Union Inn and St Mary's Church in Abbeycwmhir. □

24 The Claerwen valley

Start:	Car park at the foot of the Claerwen Reservoir dam
Distance:	8 miles (12.75 km)
Approximate time:	4 hours
Parking:	At the foot of the Claerwen Reservoir dam
Refreshments:	None
Ordnance Survey maps:	Landranger 147 (Elan Valley & Builth Wells), Pathfinder 969, SN 86/96 (Rhayader)

General description *Old tracks form the bulk of this route, which climbs from the valley of the River Claerwen to cross a windswept plateau, then descends through forest to the road running along the side of Caban-coch Reservoir. It passes the little Dolymynach dam and follows the track up the southern side of the river valley to return to the more imposing dam that holds back the water of the Claerwen Reservoir.*

Refer to map overleaf.

The mighty curved dam (**A**) which overlooks the start of this walk was constructed between 1946 and 1952. Made of mass concrete, it is faced with gritstone from South Wales and Derbyshire to appear like the older dams in the Elan valley. This one is also the highest gravity dam in Britain, being 184 feet (56 m) high and 1,166 feet (355 m) long. It holds back a reservoir some 4 miles (6.5 km) long, with a capacity of 10,625 million gallons (48,300m lit.). Such statistics are the stuff of the tourist trail around the Elan valley's reservoirs. They are only reservoirs, however. Long before they were created to supply Birmingham with water, the splendid scenery and open moorland were popular, attracting the poet Shelley and his wife Harriet in 1810.

Turn right along the access road, keeping above the River Claerwen on your right. Pass the road coming from the top of the dam on the left. Just before the road is fenced, bear left uphill along a signposted public bridleway (**B**). This is probably an ancient route, perhaps pioneered by semi-nomadic Bronze Age peoples. Just before work began on the Elan valley reservoirs in 1893, eighty head of cattle from the lowlands of Ceredigion were brought to the Claerwen valley for summer grazing. The pasture also supported herds of ponies, with pit ponies being bred in the area.

The bridleway soon bears right to run parallel with the road below. It gradually diverges from the line of the road and passes conifer trees on your right. Go across a stream and climb to walk above its valley on the left. Go left along a firm track that has come up from the top edge of the conifer plantation.

Bear left at a fork (**C**) to head towards a forest. When the firm track bends right towards a couple of windmills, go straight ahead along a grassy track, passing the forest on the left. Continue through a gate (**D**) and follow the bridleway into the forest. Bear left downhill at a track junction, as waymarked by a white arrow. Go straight ahead at a crossroads with a

Looking across the valley of the River Claerwen, near Rhiwnant

lower track and descend towards Caban-coch Reservoir. Reach the road (**E**) near the bridge that separates Caban-coch and Garreg-ddu reservoirs. Nantgwllt church, built in 1903, overlooks this bridge. Go right to walk along the road above Caban-coch Reservoir on the left and at the foot of the forest on the right.

Nantgwllt, the mansion where the Shelleys lived and which probably inspired Brett Young's novel *The House under the Water*, was drowned when Caban-coch Reservoir was created. The Elan valley belonged to Shelley's uncle, and the romantic poet hoped to retire from the world here, forming a community with friends. This could only remain a dream as he was unable to buy the property. Spiritual communities were not unknown in this place. The reservoir also flooded Dolymynach, where a house is believed to have belonged to Cistercian monks from Strata Florida Abbey (Walk 27). They owned vast estates in this area and were responsible for introducing sheep farming on a grand scale. The monks exported wool from the Elan valley to Flanders and Florence after King John

of England gave them a duty free licence in 1212. The house at Dolymynach was built of stone and richly panelled inside with oak. Many rooms had a distinct 'praying-area', complete with decorative stone altars. The dam at Dolymynach was never completed because it was superseded by the large dam further up the Claerwen valley.

The dams and reservoirs were the result of pressures on far-off Birmingham. Clean water was required for the city's expanding population and growing industry. Looking west, the city fathers noted the high annual rainfall of 70 inches (1,780 mm) on the catchment area of the Elan and Claerwen rivers as well as the area's altitude, which meant that water could travel by gravity to Birmingham without being pumped. Water could also be stored easily in the narrow valleys of impermeable bedrock. Dams would be easy to construct.

The little matter of destroying the homes and livelihoods of 400 local people was overcome by an Act of Parliament in 1892. Unlike the landowners, the small-holders and tenant farmers received no

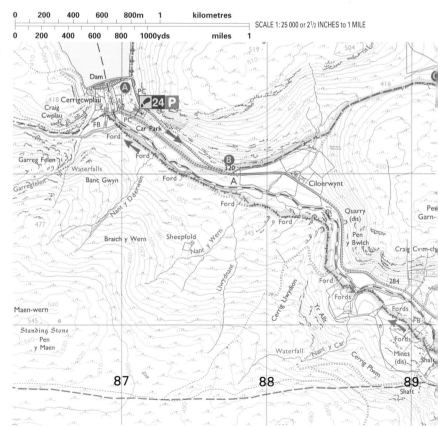

64

compensation. An army of itinerant workers soon arrived and was accommodated in doss-house huts. A model village was built for the best workers, whose first task was to lay the track of a railway. The dams had to be built with stone brought by train from near Builth Wells. The Caban-coch, Penygarreg and Craig Goch dams were commissioned in 1904, when King Edward VII performed the formal opening ceremony on 21 July. A week later, the first of the water flowed into the receiving reservoir at Birmingham. The gross storage capacity of 11,175 million gallons (50,800m lit.) sufficed until the middle of the twentieth century. The water flows for 73 miles (117 km) at an average gradient of 1 in 2,300. A submerged dam was built in Caban-coch Reservoir to hold back the water at a height of 82 feet (25 m) above the floor of the reservoir, as the aqueduct had to begin from a valve 770 feet (235 m) above sea-level, if the water was to reach Birmingham, at 600 feet (183 m), by gravity. With the opening of the Claerwen dam by Queen Elizabeth II on 23 October 1952, the gross storage capacity was increased to 21,800 million gallons (99,100m lit.). This allows Birmingham to draw off 70 million gallons (318m lit.) daily.

Fork left when you reach a telephone-box on the left (**F**). Cross the River Claerwen, then turn right and follow a lane up the valley, with the river below on the right. Ignore a waymarked bridleway going uphill on the left. Follow the lane across a bridge over a tributary stream, Rhiwnant. Pass the farm known as Rhiwnant and continue along a rough, fenced track. Bare pasture slopes uphill on your left, while the river remains below on the right. Pass a belt of conifer trees on your left, then fork right at a junction with a track that goes up the hillside on the left. Keep walking up the valley and eventually meet the River Arban, in the shadow of the Claerwen Reservoir's dam. You could follow the right-of-way by fording this river at its confluence with the River Claerwen. There is also a footbridge on the left to allow an alternative route to the other side of this river. Turn right across the bridge at the foot of the dam to return to the start of this walk at the car park. □

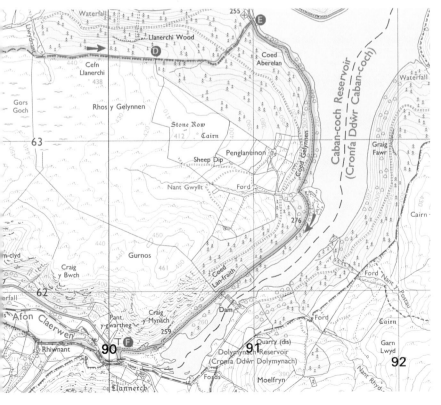

25 The Kerry Ridgeway

Start:	Kerry
Distance:	9 miles (14.5 km)
Approximate time:	4½ hours
Parking:	Kerry
Refreshments:	Pub at Kerry
Ordnance Survey maps:	Landranger 136 (Newtown & Llanidloes), Pathfinders 908, SO 09/19 (Newtown) and 929, SO 08/18 (Llandinam & Dolfor)

General description *The climb to 1,549 feet (472 m) is not as strenuous as it sounds. The gradient to the ridgeway is steady, and the lanes and tracks are firm. The views, too, are splendid, north over the rolling hills of old Montgomeryshire and south to the intriguing heights of Radnorshire. The route follows the pre-historic ridgeway for over 1 mile (1.5 km) before descending with gentle tracks and quiet lanes back to Kerry.*

Cars may be parked in The Square, which is also where the buses, from Newtown, stop. Put St Michael and All Angels' Church at your back and face the Herbert Arms. Cross the A489 road and go ahead along Common Road, passing the pub on your right. Follow the road to the edge of the village.

When the road bears right, fork left down a woodland path (**A**). This leads back to the road. Go left along it for 50 yards (46 m) and turn right up steps, through a small metal gate and past a school playing-field on your left. Descend to the road and go right. Pass a 'no through road' that soon appears on your right. Continue to a T-junction and turn right.

Fork right along a 'no through road' (**B**) which leads past Black Hall, on your right. Pass the turning for Cefn-mynach, on your right. The metalled lane ends at Lower Rhos, but maintain your direction by climbing gradually with a grassy track. This keeps to the right-hand side of pasture, then goes through a forestry plantation. Emerge to walk with trees on your right and, where they end, join the ancient Kerry Ridgeway (**C**).

Turn right to follow the firm track of this prehistoric route. Also known as Yr Hen Ffordd 'the old road', this is a fine

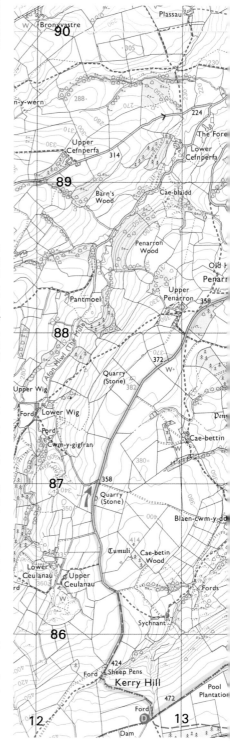

Follow the track from Lower Rhos to climb to the Kerry Ridgeway

example of an ancient ridgeway, following the crest of the Kerry Hills. Bronze Age round barrows and other evidence of our ancestors may be found near it; there is one in the forest on your right, just before attaining the ridge, but it is obscured by trees. Early stone tools dating back to about 6000 BC have been found.

Approach a ford (**D**) and turn right through a gate just before it. Follow a grassy track that crosses the stream and bears left to descend and cross a second stream before turning right. Go past sheep-pens and notice a track converging on yours from sharp left. Keep to the main track, ignoring a farm access lane on your right. Pass a second farm access lane on our left before the track turns into a metalled lane.

Descend gradually with the lane to Lower Penarron, where you ignore a lane on your left. Climb over the brow of the next hill and follow the lane around a dog-leg on your left. Fork left at a junction with your outward road and soon pass where you plunged down the woodland path (A).

Retrace your steps into Kerry. These tracks feeding into the ridgeway may be thousands of years old too.

Kerry's church (**E**) certainly has a colourful past. It probably stands on an ancient holy spot. When it was rebuilt in 1176, both the diocese of St Asaph and the diocese of St David claimed it. An unseemly row ensued which resulted in the Bishop of St Asaph and Giraldus Cambrensis of St David's excommunicating each other. Giraldus won in the end, and the Bishop had to endure stones being thrown at him by the locals. The final twist to this tale came in 1849 when the church was transferred to St Asaph without a hair being turned. Go inside the church to admire the Welsh bible, printed in Oxford in 1690, chained to the lectern. The sexton used to perambulate the church during services and wake sleepers by ringing a 'little ting tang bell'.

Sheep have played an important part in Kerry's prosperity. The Kerry Hill breed is recognised as one of the finest in Britain and won the Supreme Inter-Breed Championship at the Royal Welsh Show in 1988. Hardy and adaptable, it is covered with a fleece of white wool, except for the face and legs.

The Kerry Fair used to take place in The Square every 16 September. The many sheep were transported by rail when Kerry had its own station and branch line. Opened in 1863, they were closed in 1956. □

26 Clun

Start:	Clun
Distance:	11½ miles (18.5 km)
Approximate time:	6 hours
Parking:	Clun
Refreshments:	Pubs at Clun and at Purslow
Ordnance Survey maps:	Landranger 137 (Ludlow & Wenlock Edge, Pathfinders 930, SO 28/38 (Bishop's Castle & Clun) and 950, SO 27/37 (Knighton & Brampton Bryan)

General description *This stimulating walk takes you over the hills and through the forests in the outstandingly beautiful countryside around Clun. It follows ancient tracks and part of the Shropshire Way, and there is a pub at the midway point. Allow time to visit the ruins of the castle at Clun.*

Refer to map overleaf.

Clun Bridge car park has a tempting footbridge at its back, which gives access to the ruins of Clun Castle (**A**). This was first built by Robert de Say, known as 'Picot', shortly after the Norman Conquest. This Marcher Lord held the land of the Saxon resistance leader Eldric the Wild. The castle was later captured by ambitious Welsh princes: Lord Rhys in 1195 or 1196 and Llywelyn ap Iorwerth in 1214.

Go left from the car park entrance and turn left to cross the road bridge over the River Clun. Bear right up Bridge Street and turn right along Clun's High Street, passing the Sun Inn on the left. Turn left just after a bus-shelter, taking Ford Street. Go right, as signed for the youth hostel. Pass the old almshouses of Trinity Hospital on the right. Continue past the youth hostel on your right. When the lane swings left, bear right along a hedged track.

The track becomes an attractive hollow way as it climbs to end at a stile. Go ahead to follow the left-hand edges of three fields. Go ahead through a gate (**B**) to enter woodland. Descend near the edge of the wood, on the left, to emerge in the corner of a field. Turn right and descend to a stile above a gate. Cross it and bear left downhill to cross a stream and climb to a track (**C**). Turn right along this, at the foot of woodland on your left.

Go ahead through the farmyard at Stepple. Take the waymarked track ahead. Approach a house, which used to be two barns, as you descend to the bottom of the valley. Bear left to pass the house on the right, cross a stream and turn right to climb gradually to a stile in the hedge ahead. Continue past a cottage known as Dawes Lines on the left and follow a track to a road (**D**).

Go left for 250 yards (229 m), and turn to the right off the road down a track signposted as Wild Eldric's Way, as well as the Shropshire Way. Continue ahead along this track to a lane at Kempton, where you ignore roads on your left. Take the road ahead to the crossroads at Purslow. Go ahead to pass the Hundred House Inn on your left. Just after passing road signs indicating that the road will bend left (**E**), turn right through an iron gate to follow the signposted path past a hall on the right-hand side.

Rolling, wooded countryside on the route east of Clun

Take a gate in a fence ahead and continue to a footbridge. Cross the River Clun by it, go ahead about 100 yards (91 m), bear right over a railing, acting as a stile in the fence on your right, then bear left up this long, narrow field to go through a gate (**F**) and join a lane. Go right to walk with forest on the left. Bear left at the end of the metalled lane to climb Ladye Bank and go through delightful woodland. Climb to the top of this wooded slope, then fork right, as waymarked, to a road.

Go left up the road for ¼ mile (0.5 km) until a cluster of stiles, gates and signposts mark where paths and tracks cross it (**G**). Turn sharply right through a gate to

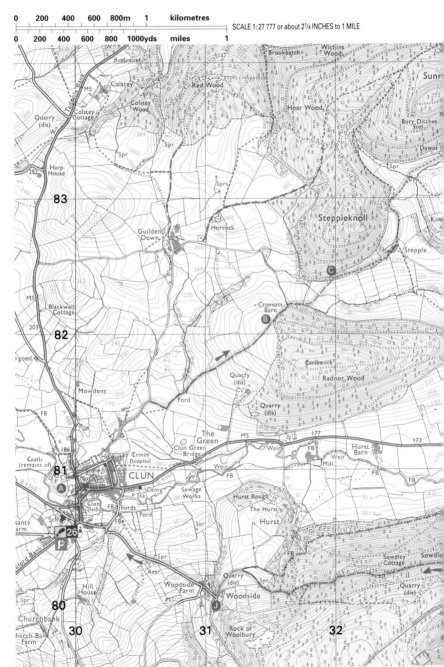

SCALE 1: 27 777 or about 2¼ INCHES to 1 MILE

follow a hedged track. Climb to a junction with a signposted public bridleway on the right (**H**) and fork right to follow this through Sowdley Wood. Keep to the main forest track and gradually descend to leave the wood and converge with another track coming from the right. Go left to reach a road (**J**).

Turn right, ignore a road on the left and pass Woodside Farm on the right. Go right with this road as it enters Clun by climbing to a junction, where you turn left to reach St George's Church, on the left. Turn right downhill towards Clun Bridge and turn left to return to the car park, with the river and the car park on the right. □

27 Teifi Pools

Start:	Strata Florida
Distance:	9½ miles (15.25 km)
Approximate time:	5 hours
Parking:	Strata Florida
Refreshments:	None
Ordnance Survey maps:	Landranger 135 (Aberystwyth) or 147 (Elan Valley & Builth Wells), Pathfinder 968, SN 66/76 (Bronnant & Pontrhydfendigaid)

General description *Allow time to visit the ruins of Strata Florida Abbey before taking a lane into the 'green desert'. The plateau is a crumpled landscape of rocky outcrops and marshy depressions. The chief features are the lakes, which have been increased in size by the construction of small dams. A metalled lane makes the route around them easy going. A grassy bridleway leads back through farmyards to the road and Strata Florida. Wild in its beauty, this walk never quite demands the physical exertions that the impressive, rugged scenery threatens.*

Strata Florida Abbey is one of the glories of mid Wales. An earlier abbey, completed by the Welsh Lord Rhys, had stood on the banks of the Afon Fflur about 2 miles (3.25 km) away, but this foundation was given to the Cistercians in 1201. The monks farmed sheep for their wool

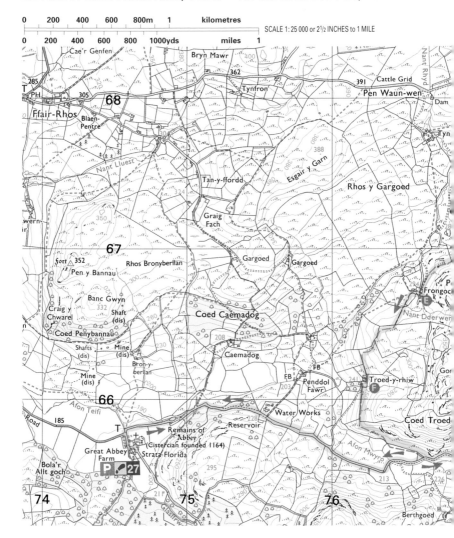

SCALE 1:25 000 or 2½ INCHES to 1 MILE

and changed the face of the countryside by converting woodland into pasture. The Dissolution found the Abbot of Strata Florida in charge of a rental income of £150 but with only six monks to support. The buildings had already suffered during the patriotic war of Owain Glyndŵr in the early fifteenth century. The property eventually found itself in the hands of the Powell family of Nanteos, near Aberystwyth, which explains their possession of the famous Nanteos Cup. Believed to be the holy grail, the chalice used at Christ's Last Supper, it was brought to Strata Florida from Glastonbury and was renowned for its miraculous healing properties.

Walk to the cemetery to see Dafydd ap Gwilym's yew tree. This supposed resting-place of Wales' greatest poet ex-cited George Borrow, the author of *Wild Wales*, when he came here in 1854. He addressed the tree thus:

Better for thee thy boughs to wave,
Though scath'd, above Ab Gwilym's grave
Than stand in pristine glory drest
Where some ignobler bard dost rest; ...

Dafydd ap Gwilym wrote better poetry in the fourteenth century, and he was not as unsuccessful with women as he suggests in his poem *Merched Llanbadarn* (The Girls of Llanbadarn), here in translation:

I am one of passion's asses,
Plague on all these parish lasses!
Though I long for them like mad,
Not one female have I had,
Not a one in all my life,
Virgin, damsel, hag or wife.

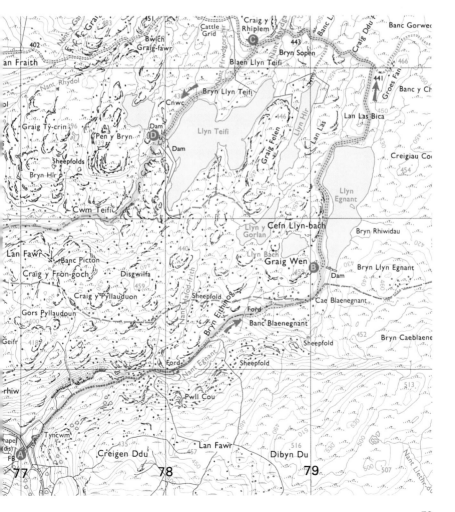

Llyn Teifi and the mid-Wales wilderness

Look for the poignant poem by local poet Evan Jenkins on the gravestone of the unknown tramp, found dead in the snow on the road to Rhayader in 1929. He was buried near princes on the ley or spirit path that links the abbey's altar with Dafydd's yew tree.

After this cautionary tale, set out for the wilderness. Facing the entrance to the abbey, go left. Ignore the road to Pont-rhydfendigaid on your left and take the road that bears right, with the River Teifi on your left.

Pass the access lane to Caemadog, then the waterworks on your left. Cross a bridge over the Afon Mwyro and pass a signposted bridleway on your left. Go ahead along the lane and reach a disused chapel on your right (**A**). Turn left, as signposted, through the farmyard of Tyncwm. Bear right uphill, as waymarked, and follow the waymarked track that keeps above a stream on your left. Keep to the higher path at a fork. Go ahead across a ford and with the waymarked track above a valley that is now on your right.

Reach the dam at the southern end of the lake known a Llyn Egnant (**B**). Go ahead along a metalled lane, passing above the lake on your right. Follow this lane to a fork (**C**) above Llyn Teifi, the lake which is the source of the River Teifi. The landscape is barren, although these slopes were densely clad by oak and birch before the Cistercians came with their flocks of sheep.

Bear left to walk above the lake on your left and follow the lane to Llyn Teifi's dam (**D**). Do not take a gate to descend with the lane towards the dam. Go to the right of it and descend with a fence on your left. Follow a path bearing right, then left, around a rocky knoll. Continue over a stile and across a stream. This is the infant River Teifi, and it remains on your right-hand side as you follow the waymarked path down the valley.

Cross a tributary stream before diverging from the Teifi by bearing left uphill with the well-trodden path. Reach the farm of Frongoch (**E**). When level with its farmhouse on your left, turn right to take a ladder-stile and go ahead to a second ladder-stile, after which you turn left, as waymarked. This firm track leads to Troed-yr-rhiw (**F**).

Do not proceed through the gate with a 'private' sign on it. Fork left, off the track, to cross a stile and take the waymarked path beside a hedge on your right and at the foot of the slope on your left. Go around the hillside, with fine views across the valley on your right. Go straight ahead, as waymarked, at a crossroads formed by another narrow path. Descend to the fence at the foot of the slope and walk with the fence on your right back to the road. Turn right to retrace your steps to Strata Florida. □

28 The source of the Severn

Start:	Rhyd-y-benwch, Hafren Forest
Distance:	8 miles (12.75 km)
Approximate time:	5 hours
Parking:	Hafren Forest, Forestry Commission car park
Refreshments:	None
Ordnance Survey maps:	Landranger 135 (Aberystwyth) or 136 (Newtown & Llanidloes), Pathfinder 928, SN 88/98 (Llanidloes)

General description Most of this route is through the Hafren Forest, where the trees are either Norway or Sitka spruce. The forest was planted in 1937, and a farmhouse called Rhyd-y-benwch once stood on the site of the car park. This is no dull walk along forest tracks past conifers, however. The young River Severn and later one of its early tributaries provide babbling company along narrow paths. A boardwalk smoothes the initial stretch, while waymark posts make navigation a simple task throughout. The route follows the white markings to climb steeply to a

The infant River Severn in Hafren Forest

high track that leads to a path from which you emerge on the high moorland plateau of Plynlimon. The way continues up the valley of the infant Severn to reach its source in a peatbog, designed to test your waterproof footwear. This is a magical spot, at around 2,000 feet (610 m) above sea-level. Returning into the forest and descending along broad, firm forest tracks, the route crosses moorland from the edge of the forest to the source of the Severn by a permissive path, where dogs must be kept on a lead. An information board at the car park at Rhyd-y-benwch shows three waymarked routes. It is easy to become lost in a forest, so do pay attention to the waymarks. The long route, the way to the source of the Severn, has white waymarks.

Refer to map overleaf.

Start by following the path down to the River Severn. This is waymarked by posts bearing all three colours: red, blue and white.

Reach a track where it fords the River Severn, on your left (**A**). Do not take this ford but go straight ahead across the track and walk with the river on your left. This part of the walk is a boardwalk to the Cascades, where there is a picnic area. Shepherds used the deep pool at the foot of the Cascades to wash their sheep.

The red waymarked route turns right, away from the river and into the forest, at this point. Do not take this but go ahead, keeping the river on your left. Pass the Severn Flume, where the discharge of the river is measured.

At a length of 220 miles (354 km), the Severn is the longest river in Britain. It also has the most romantic story. The English name Severn should really be Sabrina, as it is derived from Habren or Hafren. Habren (Sabrina) was the daughter of Locrinus, the eldest son of Brutus, who gave his name to Britain after leading the Trojans to what was then called Albion. Unfortunately, Habren's mother was Estrildis, the mistress of Locrinus, rather than Gwendolen, his wife. Locrinus originally concealed his mistress in a secret cave in London. Gwendolen was the daughter of Corineus, the follower of Brutus who was given Cornwall because he loved fighting giants, and there were more of them in Cornwall than elsewhere. It was this Corineus who hurled the giant Gogmagog to his death from Plymouth Hoe, so it would not have been wise for Locrinus to enrage his father-in-law! Then Corineus died, and Locrinus openly set aside Gwendolen to make Estrildis his queen.

Gwendolen summoned help from Cornwall and managed to defeat and kill Locrinus. Taking over the kingdom, she ordered the fleeing Estrildis and her daughter to be thrown into the river that now bears Habren's name. Habren became the river goddess addressed by Milton as 'Sitting under the glassy, cool translucent wave, in twisted braids of lilies knitting the loose train of thy amber-dropping hair'.

Come to a confluence, with the Afon Hore, where the Severn turns right (**B**). Turn right to keep the Severn on the left until you reach a footbridge across it. Turn left to go over this footbridge and im-

mediately turn right to walk with the river on the right. When the Severn takes another bend to the right, bear left with the waymarked path to enter the forest. Do not be enticed up a wide forest ride, but do follow the white and blue waymarks. Nant Tanllwyth, a tributary of the Severn, is on the right. Follow the waymarks to a footbridge across it. Turn right to cross the bridge and then turn left along the waymarked path, with the stream now on the left.

The narrow forest path eventually climbs to a broad, firm forest track (**C**). This is where the blue route turns right. The way to the source of the Severn lies

SCALE 1 : 25 000 or 2½ INCHES to 1 MILE

ahead, as waymarked in white. Cross the track to climb with this route, keeping the stream, Nant Tanllwyth, on the left. The route is well waymarked but steep in places. Climb to another firm forest track and cross it to continue as directed by the white-topped posts. The path becomes less steep and eventually reaches a higher forest track (**D**).

Turn right along this track, following the white waymarks. Ignore the first turning on the left, which is waymarked for Plynlimon. If you were to follow this route over the moorland to the 2,468-foot (752 m) summit of Plynlimon (Pumlumon Fawr), you would have a trek of at least 4 miles (6.5 km) each way. You would pass above the source of the River Wye. The Rheidol also rises on this mountain, which is described in the story of 'Culhwch and Olwen' in *The Mabinogion* as being where the Arthurian knights Cei and Bedwyr sat 'in the highest wind in the world'.

Follow the forest track as it passes above the confluence of two streams on the right. The further stream is the Severn, and you soon reach a post which says 'Source of the Severn'. Turn left here to walk with the infant River Severn on the

left. Emerge from the forest to continue with the white-topped waymark posts. These indicate a permissive path above the river in its distinct ravine on the left. When you finally reach two wooden posts, stating 'Tarddiad Afon Hafren' and 'Source of Severn', you are near the source (**E**). This is not distinct because of the peaty, boggy nature of the ground. Walking a little beyond the official posts does bring you to a small pool, out of which the first babbling brook of the Severn can be seen leaving on its long journey. The land stretching south-west-wards from here to the source of the River Wye is known as Fferllys and belongs to the fairies or *tylwyth teg*. On St John's Eve (23 June), come here to gather small blue flowers from the ferns. Use a white cloth and ensure that no hand touches them if you wish their magic to work. They make the gatherer invisible so that he or she can enter a lover's room without any compli-cations. If you prefer to surrender the seeds you have gathered to one of the resident elves, you can accept a purse of gold instead.

Retrace your steps from the source of the Severn, which is now on the right as you descend to the forest. Back on the forest track, go left and find a waymark post which states that it is 3 miles (4.75 km) back to Rhyd-y-benwch. Follow the white-topped waymark posts. Reach a crossroads (**F**) and turn right, as way-marked. Turn left with the white way-marks at the next junction. Descend to where another track comes up sharply from the right. Go ahead to find that you are back with the blue waymarks.

The trees of this forest conceal an old quarry, which British Aerospace now use for testing aviation and satellite equip-ment. This remote site is relatively free from electrical interference. It is not free of strange lights in the sky, however. These are known to pre-date British Aerospace and accompany seismic activity, as on 15 April 1984, when an inexplicable light was seen in the sky just before one of Britain's strongest earthquakes, which measured 3.3 on the Richter scale.

Shortly after a track comes in sharply from your left to join your broad track, and just before another track junction, turn sharply right at a blue waymark post (**G**). Descend with this track, which is way-marked with blue-topped posts. As you descend, ignore a track on the left. Red-topped posts lead the way down to the picnic area at the Cascades. Turn left along the boardwalk to accompany the River Severn on the right and retrace your steps to the car park at Rhyd-y-benwch. □

Useful organisations

Cadw (Welsh Historic Monuments)
Brunel House, 2 Fitzalan Road,
Cardiff CF2 1UY.
Tel: 01222 500200

Campaign for the Protection of Rural Wales
Tŷ Gwyn, 31 High Street,
Welshpool, Powys SY21 7JP.
Tel: 01938 552525

Countryside Commission
John Dower House,
Crescent Place, Cheltenham,
Gloucestershire GL50 3RA.
Tel: 01242 521381

Countryside Council for Wales
Plas Penrhos, Ffordd Penrhos,
Bangor, Gwynedd LL5 72LQ.
Tel: 01248 370444

Forestry Commission
Information Branch,
231 Corstorphine Road,
Edinburgh EH12 7AT.
Tel: 0131 334 0303

Long Distance Walkers' Association
7 Ford Drive, Yarnfield,
Stone, Staffordshire ST15 0RP

Ordnance Survey
Romsey Road, Maybush,
Southampton SO16 4GU.
Tel: 01703 792912

Ramblers' Association
Tŷ'r Cerddwyr, High Street,
Gresford, Wrexham, Clwyd LL12 8PT.
Tel: 01978 855148

Tourist information centres in this area (*not
open all year):
Aberystwyth, Terrace Road. Tel: 01970
612125
*Borth, Hight Street. Tel: 01970 871174
*Builth Wells, Groe Car Park. Tel: 01982
553307
*Elan Valley Visitor Centre, Rhayader.
Tel: 01597 810898
Hereford, Town Hall Annexe, St Owen's Street.
Tel: 01432 268430
Knighton, The Offa's Dyke Centre, West Street.
Tel: 01547 528753
*Leominster, 1 Corn Square. Tel: 01568
616460
*Llandiloes, Longbridge Street. Tel: 01686
412605
Llandrindod Wells, Old Town Hall, Memorial
Gardens. Tel: 01597 822600
Ludlow, Castle Street. Tel: 01584 875053
Machynlleth, Canolfan Owain Glyndŵr.
Tel: 01654 702401
*Newtown, Museum and Art Gallery, John
Frost Square. Tel: 01686 625580
*Presteigne, The Old Market Hall, Broad Street.
Tel: 01544 260193
*Rhayader, North Street. Tel: 01597 810591
Tregaron, The Square. Tel: 01974 298144
Welshpool, The Flash Leisure Centre.
Tel: 01938 552043

Youth Hostels Association
Trevelyan House, 8 St Stephen's Hill,
St Albans, Hertfordshire AL1 2DY.
Tel: 01727 855215

Wales Tourist Board
Brunel House, 2 Fitzalan Road,
Cardiff CF2 1UY.
Tel: 01222 499909

Weather forecasts:
For Wales, 48-hour forecast. Tel: 0891 112265
UK seven-day forecast. Tel: 0891 333123

Ordnance Survey maps of mid Wales and the Marches

The walks described in this guide are covered by Ordnance Survey 1:50 000 scale (1¼ inches to 1 mile or 2 cm to 1 km) Landranger map sheets 125, 135, 136, 137, 138, 146, 147, 148, 149, 160 and 161.

These all-purpose maps are packed with information to help you explore the areas. Viewpoints, picnic sites, places of interest and caravan and camping sites are shown as well as public rights-of-way information such as footpaths and bridleways.

To examine this area in more detail, and especially if you are planning walks, the Ordnance Survey Pathfinder maps at 1:25 000 scale (2½ inches to 1 mile or 4 cm to 1 km) are ideal. Maps covering the area are:

887 (SJ 00/10)	969 (SN 86/96)
907 (SN 89/99)	970 (SO 06/16)
908 (SO 09/19)	971 (SO 26/36)
926 (SN 57/58)	972 (SO 46/56)
927 (SN 68/78)	990 (SN 65/75)
928 (SN 88/98)	991 (SN 85/95)
929 (SO 08/18)	992 (SO 05/15)
930 (SO 28/38)	993 (SO 25/35)
947 (SN 67/77)	994 (SO 45/55)
948 (SN 87/97)	1013 (SN 64/74)
949 (SO 07/17)	1014 (SN 84/94)
950 (SO 27/37)	1015 (SO 04/14)
968 (SN 66/76)	1017 (SO 44/54)

To get to mid Wales and the Marches use the Ordnance Survey Great Britain Routeplanner (Travelmaster map number 1) or Travelmaster maps 7, Wales and West Midlands, and 8, South West England and South Wales.

Ordnance Survey maps and guides are available from most booksellers, stationers and newsagents.

Index